50
ethics ideas
you really need to know

Ben Dupré

Quercus

Contents

Introduction

Ethics is about right and wrong – about what we should and shouldn't do. What are the principles that should guide our behaviour? What are the values we should live by? What, in the end, is the purpose and meaning of life?

These are profound questions, though we may think that we already have some of the answers. We all know that it is wrong to kill. Or do we? Murderers kill other people – that is wrong – but is it right that we kill murderers to punish them? Soldiers kill others with the blessing of the state: does that authority make killing in time of war acceptable? Then there are issues such as euthanasia and the widespread slaughter of animals: an array of cases that cast doubt on the claim that killing is always wrong.

Questions about what we should do and be are fundamental to our human nature – we are profoundly, essentially ethical creatures – so such questions are as old as mankind. 'If I have seen a little further,' Isaac Newton famously observed, 'it is by standing on the shoulders of giants.' In the field of ethics, our vision would be greatly impaired without the insights offered by the philosophical giants of the past – Plato, Aristotle, Kant, Bentham, Mill – as well as by their more recent successors. Yet no work by these philosophers has rivalled the Bible or the Qur'an in its influence on human behaviour. And in the inevitable conflict of values, religion and philosophy often reach strikingly different conclusions.

This book explores some of the most important ethical issues, taking into account the insights provided by both religious and secular thinkers. If the emphasis is very much on Western thinking, that is a reflection of the constraints of space and my own competence. The ideas discussed are endlessly engaging because they challenge not just the way we think but the way we act – because, ultimately, they really matter. My hope is that they rattle your conscience as you read about them, just as they have mine in the course of writing.

Ben Dupré

01 The good life

How should we live in order to live a good life? What is it that makes our lives valuable? These most basic of ethical questions were first posed in ancient Greece some 25 centuries ago. Since then they have never ceased to divide opinions or the people who hold them.

Views on what constitutes the good life have covered the broadest spectrum. And in this case, unfortunately, difference of opinion really matters. For starkly divergent views on the good life more or less directly affect how we actually behave and interact with one another as social beings. Much human suffering has flowed from disagreement on these basic questions.

THROUGH A VALE OF TEARS

From a religious perspective, a good life is one lived in accordance with the will and wishes of a particular god or gods. In the case of Christianity, the reward for a life well spent is a blissful afterlife in which to dwell with God for eternity. The source of true value therefore lies outside this world. To a significant degree, what we do and achieve on Earth is valuable in a secondary, instrumental sense, to the extent that it helps us to gain admission to another, infinitely better life after death.

The subordination of the physical (and inferior) here-and-now to the spiritual (and superior) hereafter inevitably leads to elevation of the soul and demotion of the body and its accoutrements. From a Christian viewpoint, our earthly life is a time of sorrow, a passage through a 'vale of tears', where our

TIMELINE

5th century BC	4th century BC	4th–3rd century BC
In Athens, Socrates asks 'How should we live?'	Aristotle affirms that happiness (*eudaimonia*) is the highest good	Epicurus advocates pleasure as the highest good

mundane hopes are transitory, our petty ambitions empty. Virtue is to be found primarily in obedience to the will of God, a devotion that, historically at least, has often been accompanied by disdain for worldly goods. The qualities that have traditionally been encouraged by the Church are habits of dedication and self-denial, such as chastity, abstinence and humility.

> **BLESSED ARE THE POOR IN SPIRIT: FOR THEIRS IS THE KINGDOM OF HEAVEN … BLESSED ARE THE PURE IN HEART: FOR THEY SHALL SEE GOD.**
>
> Jesus Christ,
> Sermon on the Mount, C.AD 30

HAPPINESS, AUTONOMY AND REASON

Non-religious thinkers, without expectation of an afterlife, are obliged to lower their gaze, taking a humanist (in other words, human-centred) perspective and locating whatever value life may have, whatever scope and promise it may offer, within this world – in the natural world, that is, including the people who inhabit it.

The ancient Greeks (who had gods but did not generally aspire to live with them) and many since have regarded happiness as the 'highest good'

Aristotle on the good life

For the Greek philosopher Aristotle, like Socrates and Plato before him, the critical ethical question was not so much 'What is the right thing to do?' but 'What is the best way to live?'. He accepted the usual Greek view that man's highest good is *eudaimonia*: generally translated as 'happiness' but closer in meaning to 'flourishing' – a more objective, less psychological state than the word 'happiness' suggests, comprising success, fulfilment, self-realization and an adequate level of material comfort. As Aristotle believed that man's essence is his ability to reason, the fulfilment of his distinctively human potential, and hence his *eudaimonia*, consists in 'the active exercise of the soul's faculties [i.e. rational activity] in conformity with virtue or moral excellence'.

C.AD 30	1784	1789	1983
Jesus promises the faithful that their reward is in heaven	Immanuel Kant argues that freedom and reason are the key to human progress	Jeremy Bentham maintains that happiness is the one true measure of value	Monty Python's *The Meaning of Life* confounds both Jesus and Kant

The meaning of life

Monty Python concluded that it was 'nothing very special': 'try and be nice to people, avoid eating fat, read a good book every now and then ...' But for most people the question of whether life has meaning – and if so, what it might be – seems like a seriously and/or alarmingly Big Question. For the religious, the answer may be relatively straightforward: we are put on Earth for a purpose, to serve and glorify God. Those without religion, however, are obliged to find comfort elsewhere (*see also chapter 21*). Many atheists agree with the existentialist Jean-Paul Sartre, who argued that the very fact of the universe's indifference to us (indifferent because there is no God to give purpose to our lives) leaves us free to engage with the world in ways that create meaning for us. 'Condemned to be free', we are what we choose to be, products of the significant choices we make and authors of meaning in our lives.

(*summum bonum*) of human beings. There has been a wide range of views, however, on the nature of happiness and how it is to be achieved. For example, the Greek philosopher Epicurus identified happiness with pleasure (though not the kind of sensual pleasure now usually associated with his name), as did, much later, Jeremy Bentham, the pioneer of utilitarianism (*see also chapter 12*), for very different purposes. Others, while agreeing that happiness is the (or perhaps a) supreme good, have followed Aristotle in seeing it as an objective state of human flourishing or well-being, rather than as a subjective state of mind.

Socrates famously claimed that the unconsidered life is not worth living. It is essential, according to this line of thought, that we think for ourselves and constantly reflect on what makes our lives valuable. Otherwise, we risk living, not by values that we choose for ourselves, but by those imposed on us by others. This insight proved inspirational to a succession of thinkers during the Enlightenment, notably Immanuel Kant (*see also chapter 13*), who proclaimed that personal autonomy, and especially freedom of thought and expression, were essential if human beings were to escape the shackles of superstition and deference to traditional authority.

The thirst for knowledge that consumed Enlightenment thinkers was stimulated in large part by the demands of freedom and autonomy. Courage to act and decide on our own account depends on understanding the context and implications of our actions and decisions. Reason was recognized (again, as the Greeks had done) as the midwife of such boldness. And in practice the pioneers of the scientific revolution, from Newton to Darwin, devised and developed methods of experimentation and rationally based inquiry that would bring undreamed-of insight into the physical world and man's place within it.

NOTHING IS REQUIRED FOR THIS ENLIGHTENMENT EXCEPT FREEDOM ... THE FREEDOM TO USE REASON PUBLICLY IN ALL MATTERS.

Immanuel Kant,
What is Enlightenment?, 1784

WORLDS APART

Today, as much as ever in the past, there is a vast gulf between those who see human life as a moment of transition to a better existence hereafter and those who, like the ancient Greeks, 'make man the measure of all things' and seek to realize the potential of human beings within the confines of a finite life on Earth. We humans are, literally, worlds apart in our understanding of our origins and nature – where we come from and the implications this has for the manner in which we live our lives. Sadly, until we can reach some consensus on what makes a good life good, there is little prospect of accommodation in the more down-to-earth business of getting along peacefully in the world.

The condensed idea
What is the best way to live?

02 Divine command

Of all the people who have ever lived, now and in the past, the great majority have believed that human beings are products of divine creation. Details of the connection between creature and creator differ from religion to religion, but commonly something akin to a parent–child relationship is supposed. And just as most would agree that a child's behaviour should be guided by its parents, so our behaviour as humans (so believers believe) should be directed by the will of God or the gods.

Specifically, each of the three 'religions of the Book' – Judaism, Christianity and Islam – claims that morality is based on divine command. The principal means by which the deity's wishes are made known to human beings is through sacred scriptures, notably the Bible and Qur'an, which are believed to be divinely inspired or the directly revealed word of God. So, according to this view, a thought or deed is right or wrong because God has ordained that it is so; virtue lies in obedience to God's will, while disobedience is sin.

THE EUTHYPHRO DILEMMA

Moral codes based on divine command may be very widely adopted, but nevertheless they face some difficulties. The most fundamental is the existence of God: is there in reality a deity to issue commands? This question is perhaps the least likely to be resolved, however, as the parties to the dispute, believers on one side and non-believers on the other, come armed with different weapons: faith and reason.

TIMELINE

?18th century BC	4th century BC
Abraham is ordered by God to sacrifice his son Isaac	In Athens, Plato's Socrates discusses the meaning of piety with *Euthyphro*

Even setting aside this most basic question, there is another significant problem that was first raised by the Greek philosopher Plato some 2,400 years ago in his dialogue *Euthyphro*. Suppose that moral injunctions can be identified with divine commands. Is what is morally good good because God commands it, or does God command it because it is good?

If the former is the case, clearly God's preferences might have been different. God *might* have ordained that the innocent should be killed, for instance, and if he had, such killing would have been morally right – just because God said so. (Indeed, the Old Testament patriarch Abraham seems to have taken precisely this view in deciding that it was right to sacrifice his young son Isaac.) Morality, on this reading, comes to little more than obedience to an arbitrary authority.

Does the other alternative fare any better? Not really. If God commands what is good because it is good, clearly its goodness is independent of God. In this case, God seems to be no more than an intermediary. In principle, therefore, we could act on our own account and go straight to the moral source or standard, without God's help. So, when it comes to moral authority, it seems that God is either arbitrary or redundant.

The problem of evil

One reason sometimes put forward to explain why we should do as God tells us is that he is both good and omniscient: he has our best interests at heart, and because he knows and foresees all things, his guidance is bound to be the best guidance possible. The problem here is that the record on the ground, as it were, leaves plenty of room to doubt whether God really does have our best interests at heart. Indeed, the presence of evil in the world is one of the gravest challenges facing those who believe in God – or at least those who accept the orthodox view of God as omniscient, omnipotent and omnibenevolent. Is not the ghastly catalogue of pain and suffering in the world – famine, murder, earthquake and disease – hard to reconcile with the existence of an all-powerful, all-knowing and benevolent god? How can such evil exist side by side with a god who has, by definition, the capacity to put an end to it?

4th–3rd century BC

The problem of evil is, reputedly, first stated by the Greek philosopher Epicurus

1546

Martin Luther denounces reason as the 'Devil's greatest whore'

The fickle commander

A major difficulty for the divine command theory of ethics is that God's will, as it is revealed through numerous religious texts, contains many messages that are either unsavoury or actually contradictory. Such conflicts occur both between and within religions. To take a notorious example, the Bible (Leviticus 20:13) states: 'If a man lies with a male as with a woman, both of them have committed an abomination; they shall surely be put to death.' The recommendation that sexually active homosexuals should be executed, abhorrent in itself, contradicts injunctions against killing elsewhere in the Bible, including of course one of the Ten Commandments. At the very least, it is a challenge to use God's known views to construct an acceptable and internally coherent moral system.

DRIVING OUT THE DEVIL'S WHORE

It is hard to escape Plato's conclusion, but theologians and philosophers have responded to it in very different ways. One theological response is to insist that God is good and therefore would never command evil. But what is it to do evil, on the divine command view, other than to act in defiance of God's will? So to determine what evil is, we are no less dependent on a standard of goodness that is independent of God. And in any case, if 'good' *means* 'commanded by God', the statement 'God is good' is all but meaningless – something like 'God is such that he complies with his own commands.'

THE GOOD CONSISTS IN ALWAYS DOING WHAT GOD WILLS AT ANY PARTICULAR MOMENT.

Emil Brunner,
The Divine Imperative, 1932

The most robust response to Plato's dilemma is that made by Martin Luther, leader of the 16th-century Protestant Reformation, who insisted that the good is, indeed, whatever God commands, and that his will cannot be justified or explained by reference to any independent standard of goodness. Notoriously, Luther condemned human reason as the 'Devil's greatest whore' – as a faculty that is hostile to God, corrupt, and thus incapable of bringing a true understanding of the relationship between God and human beings.

MORALITY BEYOND REASON

Luther's view in this regard is quite consistent. If morality is based on God's authority, that authority, being arbitrary, must be taken on trust: it is beyond reason – irrational, or at least non-rational. On this view, reason is quite irrelevant in matters of morality; there is no basis for moral debate or argument, and hence, of course, no place for moral philosophy.

It is little surprise, then, that the mainstream philosophical tradition has found the other prong of Plato's dilemma less uncomfortable. Although the majority of philosophers before the 20th century believed in God or gods, or at least professed to do so, religious belief has not generally played a foundational or indispensable role in the very broad range of ethical views presented.

Reason cannot prove that human morality is not based on divine authority. What seems clear, however, is that if it is so based, we cannot know about it in the same way that we know about other things in the world. There is no way, even in principle, to decide between different religious moralities, because there are no independent criteria on which to base a decision. With rational inquiry ruled out and no evidence available, any morality seems to be as good or bad as another. That is why, for better or worse, religious morality, like religion itself, is a matter not of reason but of faith.

> **NO MORALITY CAN BE FOUNDED ON AUTHORITY, EVEN IF THE AUTHORITY WERE DIVINE.**
>
> A. J. Ayer,
> British philosopher

The condensed idea
Good because God says so?

03 Right and wrong

Is it right to use human embryos in medical research that may save lives in the future? Or to fight a war in a just cause even if it brings about the deaths of innocent civilians? Is it wrong for some people to live in affluence while others elsewhere are starving? Or for non-human animals to be slaughtered in order to provide food for human beings?

Questions of right and wrong – of what is morally good and morally bad – are the central concern of ethics, or moral philosophy. A pivotal issue in ethics is value: the moral significance or worth we attach to things. To say that something has value, in this sense, is to acknowledge that it has weight in the choices and decisions we make and that it should (other things being equal) guide our behaviour. The trouble is that other things are almost never equal.

WHEN VALUES CLASH

Values conflict, prompting moral debate and setting up moral dilemmas. To take the example of research involving human embryos: almost everyone attaches substantial value to human life; and almost everyone thinks that human beings should not be 'used' – exploited or (as Kant would put it) treated only as a means to an end. These values seem to conflict in this kind of research, however. The aim is clearly to save or improve lives; and yet human beings, arguably, are exploited in the process. We are pulled in different directions, with apparently compelling reasons both to support such research and to oppose it.

TIMELINE

1785	1940s
Immanuel Kant declares that humanity should never be treated merely as a means to an end	Emotivist view of ethics is stated by A. J. Ayer, C. L. Stevenson and others

Ethical origins

The origins of human morality must inevitably remain a matter of speculation, hidden in the depths of our prehistoric past. Still, studies of closely related non-human apes suggest how a basic sense of right and wrong might have arisen as the product of evolutionary pressures on intelligent animals living together in relatively stable social groups. In such groups, the evolutionary benefits of reciprocity and cooperation in activities such as grooming and food-gathering depend on minimizing cheating – individuals gaining benefits without returning them. And the best way to stop such skulduggery, it seems, is for offending individuals to be recognized and prevented from 'reoffending' by punishment or exclusion from the group. It does not take a huge leap of imagination to see how rudimentary ideas of fairness and cheating, right and wrong, punishment and blame could emerge from such social interactions.

In this case, as so often, it is not so much the values themselves that are at issue: it is mainly the facts of the matter that are in dispute. Specifically, it is the status of human embryos – a factual issue, albeit a thorny one – that divides opinions. Such embryos are certainly human, but are they human beings, or 'proper' human beings? Can they sensibly be described as 'people'? Or are they only potential human beings? The answers to these questions will determine, we hope, the level of consideration that embryos are entitled to – perhaps, the rights that they have (or 'enjoy', which brings out the paradoxical aspect).

> THE REALLY DIFFICULT MORAL ISSUES ARISE, NOT FROM A CONFRONTATION OF GOOD AND EVIL, BUT FROM A COLLISION BETWEEN TWO GOODS.
>
> Irving Kristol, US journalist and writer, 1983

And from there, we may be able to judge the consideration they deserve side by side with such issues as the concern due to the people whose lives will be saved or enhanced as a result of the research.

1960s

Practical (applied) questions of ethics become the focus of consistent philosophical attention

2000

The Clinton administration issues guidelines on federal funding of human embryonic stem-cell research

Of actions and spanners

When we talk about the 'right' spanner (wrench), we are not ascribing an *intrinsic* quality to it. Rather, we are saying that its jaws are the correct size to fit a particular nut – that it has a certain property (a relational, non-intrinsic property) that makes it the right tool *for the job*. It makes no sense to say that the spanner is right in itself; its rightness depends on its suitability in answering a particular human need or interest. A hurricane of philosophical hot air has been expelled in attempts to decide, basically, if what goes for spanners goes for actions too. Is killing, say, wrong intrinsically, in itself? Or do we need to consider the context and outcome of an act of killing (only? as well?) in order to decide whether it is right or wrong? Does a good deed need a naughty world in order to shine?

CLIMBING THE IVORY TOWER

One conclusion we may draw from the embryos case is that ethical issues, typically, matter and are of practical significance. For the non-sociopathic majority, the upshot of accepting that something is morally right or wrong is that we recognize that we may have to do something about it. If research involving human embryos is wrong, we should change not only what we think but what we do.

The point that ethics is centrally about real-world issues might seem too obvious to need making, were it not for the fact that philosophers themselves have sometimes appeared to forget it. For the first half of the 20th century, Anglo-American philosophy virtually gave up on the task of addressing substantive, practical moral issues. At a time when the world was almost literally falling down around them, many philosophers convinced themselves that their role was limited *in principle* to analysing the meaning of moral terms; instead of addressing questions of what is actually right and wrong, they focused on what it means to call something right or wrong.

This fascination with meta-ethics ('second-order' ethics) was due in large part to a kind of moral scepticism that set in at this time. Particularly influential in this regard was a group of philosophers called emotivists, who claimed that moral terms did not express statements of fact at all but instead expressed the emotional states of their speakers. They argued that moral statements could never, even in principle, be (or be shown to be) true or false; there were no moral truths, no moral facts, and (whatever they were) they were not the kind of things that we could have knowledge of (*see also chapter 5*).

BACK TO REALITY

In the 1960s moral philosophy was dragged back down to earth, into the real world of the Vietnam War, the struggle for civil rights and women's liberation. Since that time philosophers (most of them, some of the time) have applied their minds to the real issues of the day, embracing a wide spectrum of topics, from war and world poverty, rights and equality, to animal rights, the environment and medical ethics.

The condensed idea
Back to ethical basics

04 Moral realism

The world is an external reality that exists independently of us. At any one time there is, in principle, a unique description of how things stand in the world, and a true statement about the world is one that corresponds with that description. It is the task of science, in particular, to discover what is 'out there' – to filter out the distortions of the human perspective in order to give an accurate and objective account of the way things are. The world may look different from different points of view, but in reality it remains the same – our perspectives change but it does not.

This is a realist picture of the world, and its essential feature is objectivity: it assumes that things really exist, that they do so independently of us, and that claims made about them may be true or false. It is a common view, even a commonsense view, to which most people would broadly assent. Difficulties begin to emerge, however, when properties such as colour and sound are introduced into the picture. We may unthinkingly suppose that a tomato, unobserved, is really red, or that a falling tree, unheard, really makes a noise, but the oddity of thinking that such properties exist *independently* of human beings is obvious enough.

Matters become even more peculiar when we come to values, aesthetic or ethical. We may say that beauty is in the eye of the beholder, but we normally suppose that it is something more than that; we certainly *talk* as if it were a real property of the people and objects we describe as beautiful. Just the same

TIMELINE

4th century BC

Plato relates ethical value
to the world of Forms

1903

Modern intuitionism is
developed in G. E. Moore's
Principia Ethica

kind of concerns surround moral values. We habitually suppose that these are real and that there is more to, say, deliberate cruelty being wrong than our thinking it so. But perplexities arise when we come to consider what exactly this 'more' might amount to.

THE FURNITURE OF THE UNIVERSE

In its most robust form, the moral realist's claim is that ethical values are objective moral facts: entities that are in some sense part of the 'furniture' of the universe, or properties that are woven into its 'fabric'. As such, they have a status that is essentially the same as the physical objects of science. The distinctive feature of these entities is that they carry some kind of practical and prescriptive force – they are action-guiding, in the sense that to understand the wrongness of cruelty is to recognize a compulsion not to act cruelly. It is the sheer oddity, or 'queerness', of such entities, endowed with such strange properties, that prompts moral sceptics such as the Australian philosopher J. L. Mackie to argue that the idea of objective morality is simply an illusion.

The first and most uncompromising of all moral realists, Plato, was quite untroubled by thoughts of queerness. He constructed (or discovered, as a Platonist would say) a whole suite of metaphysical furniture: the world of Forms – a realm of perfect, unchanging and universal entities that exist outside time and space. It is somehow by imitating the Form of Justice that just things are just; by imitating the Form of Good that good things are good. Plato recognized the action-guiding aspect of these moral paradigms, claiming that it was impossible to know the Good without doing good.

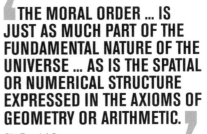

THE MORAL ORDER ... IS JUST AS MUCH PART OF THE FUNDAMENTAL NATURE OF THE UNIVERSE ... AS IS THE SPATIAL OR NUMERICAL STRUCTURE EXPRESSED IN THE AXIOMS OF GEOMETRY OR ARITHMETIC.

Sir David Ross,
The Right and the Good, 1930

1977

J. L. Mackie elaborates
his argument from
queerness

1985

Bernard Williams argues for
the personal point of view
in ethics

INTUITION AND THE NATURALISTIC FALLACY

A difficult challenge for moral realists is to explain how we humans can gain access to objective moral facts, even supposing that such peculiar entities exist. Plato believed that philosophical reflection would lead the soul to recollect knowledge of the Forms that it had acquired before being born into a physical body. For most, Plato's account will do more to highlight the difficulty of the question than to provide a satisfactory answer. Seeking a less (slightly less) exotic means of salvaging moral realism, various realists at various times have suggested that people have an innate moral sense or faculty, a kind of 'intuition', that allows them to grasp objective moral facts directly.

One of the modern pioneers of ethical intuitionism, the English philosopher G. E. Moore, is best remembered today for his discussion of what he called the 'naturalistic fallacy'. Many before him, he argued, had made the mistake of trying to *reduce* moral properties to natural ones. So, for instance, the early utilitarians tried to define 'good' as 'whatever promotes happiness'. But such a move is bound to fail, in Moore's view, because it is always an open, meaningful question to ask, 'OK, but is whatever promotes happiness itself good?' In other words, analysing goodness in terms of some other property (happiness, pleasure, duty, etc.) will only ever shift the problem onto that other property. Trying to explain goodness in terms of something else is as fruitless as trying to describe yellowness to a blind person. We can explain what yellowness is only by pointing to something and saying, 'This is yellow'; in the same way, in the case of goodness, we can only point to something and say, 'This is good.'

Naturalism under attack

A naturalist believes that everything belongs in the world of nature and hence that everything, including ethical thinking, can ultimately be explained in natural (scientific) terms. One version of naturalism, which seeks to *identify* ethical terms (such as 'right') with natural ones (such as 'giving pleasure'), is attacked by G. E. Moore as committing the so-called naturalistic fallacy. Another version maintains that ethical conclusions can be logically drawn from non-ethical (that is, natural) premises. This latter view was questioned by the Scottish philosopher David Hume, whose famous 'guillotine' appears to sever the world of fact from the world of value. How, he asks, can we possibly move from a *descriptive* statement about how things stand in the world (an 'is' statement) to a *prescriptive* statement telling us what ought to be done (an 'ought' statement)?

Goodness and other moral properties, then, cannot be defined or analysed or identified with anything else; nor can they be proved or tested like the physical facts of science. They can be grasped only by intuition – our innate ability to apprehend that certain things are self-evidently valuable. Among the things that intuition grasps in this way, Moore himself counted friendship and beauty. Tellingly, though, subsequent intuitionists have found other things no less valuable and no less self-evident – a lack of agreement that threatens the credibility of the intuitionist approach.

THE COST OF UNIVERSALITY

Another route to moral objectivity, more subtle than the morality-as-furniture-of-the-universe variant, was traced (only to be rejected) by the English philosopher Bernard Williams. According to this view, objectivity relates not to the 'objects of morality' (the notional facts or properties that exist independently in the world) but to the validity of the reasoning that supports practical moral judgments – judgments about what we should do. Just as science (according to a common view) attempts to approximate ever closer to the objective truth by systematically eliminating the biases of the personal point of view, so too can ethical reasoning aspire to reach objective moral truth by detecting and compensating for the distortions introduced by personal or parochial concerns.

Objectivity of this kind is claimed, implicitly at least, by any ethical theory built on foundations of universality and impartiality. Williams himself, however, found the ambition of erasing the personal point of view from the business of making practical moral decisions absurd. The personal concerns, projects and commitments that are thereby excluded are precisely those things that give life much of its value and meaning: the price paid for objectivity, in this sense, is loss of individual integrity (*see chapter 30*).

The condensed idea
Values and the
furniture of the universe

Moral subjectivism

'Take any action allowed to be vicious: Wilful murder, for instance. Examine it in all lights, and see if you can find that matter of fact, or real existence, which you call vice ... The vice entirely escapes you, as long as you consider the object. You never can find it, till you turn your reflection into your own breast, and find a sentiment of disapprobation, which arises in you, towards this action. Here is a matter of fact; but it is the object of feeling, not of reason. It lies in yourself, not in the object.' (David Hume)

Before the 18th century, the great majority of thinkers, for the most part religiously inspired, believed in some or other form of moral objectivism. Then, in the Enlightenment, as religion began to loosen its hold, people began to seriously address the question of the 'foundation of morals': whether moral principles are a 'matter of fact, or real existence' – that is, objectively in the world and discoverable by reason, or rather, whether they are somehow based on the emotional responses of human beings. Modern forms of the latter view, known as moral subjectivism, are greatly indebted to the Scottish philosopher David Hume, whose influential argument, partly quoted above, appears in his *A Treatise of Human Nature*, published in 1739–40.

NAÏVE SUBJECTIVISM

For many recent philosophers, as it was for Hume, the move to a subjectivist view of morality was prompted initially by the sheer oddity of supposing that values are somehow 'out there' in the world, entities existing independently of humans who hold them valuable. At the same time, ample empirical evidence of ethical disagreement, both within and between cultures, seemed to count strongly against the idea that moral values had some kind of objective and universal status.

> **THERE IS NOTHING EITHER GOOD OR BAD, BUT THINKING MAKES IT SO.**
> Shakespeare, *Hamlet*, c.1602

An extreme reaction to such full-blown objectivism is an equally full-blown subjectivism, according to which moral assertions are simply descriptions or reports of our feelings about actions and agents. So when I say 'Murder is wrong', I am merely stating my disapproval of it. The shortcomings of this view are obvious enough. Whatever I say, provided it is an accurate description of my feelings, will be true (for me) – sincerity alone is apparently sufficient as a moral justification. So if I sincerely believe murder is right, then that is true (for me). Clearly there is no place here for moral disagreement or debate.

THE BOO/HOORAH THEORY

A more sophisticated form of subjectivism is emotivism, a theory developed by the English philosopher A. J. Ayer and others during the first half of the 20th century. According to this view (humorously called the 'boo/hoorah theory'), moral judgments are not descriptions or statements of our feelings about things in the world but *expressions*

Reason, slave of the passions

David Hume's own understanding of moral action is that all humans are naturally moved by a 'moral sense' or 'sympathy', which is essentially a capacity to share the feelings of happiness or misery of others; and it is this sentiment, in his view, rather than reason, that ultimately provides the motive for our moral actions. Reason is essential in understanding the consequences of our actions and in rationally planning how to achieve our moral aims, but it is itself inert and unable to provide any impetus to action: in Hume's famous phrase, 'reason is, and ought only to be the slave of the passions'. The precise role of reason in reaching ethical judgments has continued to hold a central and contentious place in ethics.

1936

A. J. Ayer develops the notion of emotivist ethics in his *Language, Truth and Logic*

1952

R. M. Hare gives a prescriptivist account of morality in *The Language of Morals*

Postmodernism and Nietzsche

Since the 1960s a range of postmodernist thinkers have attacked the idea of objectivity in many areas, including ethics. Suspicion of the objective and universal, seen as a construction of over-optimistic scientists and philosophers in the post-Enlightenment world, is traced back to the work of Friedrich Nietzsche, who believed that all human beliefs, far from mirroring reality, were necessarily grounded in some or other perspective on it. A particular moral code, according to this view, is only ever one among many interpretations and hence can never be true or false, right or wrong. Such a code can be understood only through the prism of its history and the psychology of its adherents. So, for instance, the 'slave morality' of the Judaeo-Christian tradition must be seen in the light of its feeble and fearful adherents. The kind of strong personality revered by Nietzsche would reject such a morality and create one of his own.

of those feelings. So, when we make a moral judgment, we are expressing an emotional response – our approbation ('hoorah!') or disapprobation ('boo!') of something in the world. 'Killing is wrong' is an expression of our disapproval ('boo to murder!'); 'it is good to tell the truth' is an expression of our approval ('hoorah for truth-telling!').

Still, we may wonder whether emotivism fares much better than naïve subjectivism. Does emotivism come any closer to accommodating the commonsense view that presupposes an external world of objective values? Emotivists may avoid having to say that 'murder is right' is true (for me) provided that that is my sincere feeling on the matter, but they do so, against the common view, only by insisting that moral assertions, as expressions of approval and disapproval, are neither true nor false. Nor does the theory sit well with the kind of debate and deliberation that characterize our actual moral lives. Moral reasoning, it seems, is little more than an exercise in rhetoric – morality as advertising, as it has been sarcastically put. Emotivists may, of course, reply that it is our commonsense assumptions that are in error, not their theory, but that is a high price to pay.

THE LOGIC OF PRESCRIPTION

Succeeding where emotivism fails – in capturing the patterns of logic that underpin ethical discourse – is considered among the chief merits of its influential subjectivist rival, prescriptivism. Closely associated with the English philosopher R. M. Hare, prescriptivism's eponymous insight is that ethical judgments have a prescriptive element – they are action-guiding, telling us what to do or how to behave. Saying that killing is wrong is to issue a moral imperative, equivalent to giving and accepting a command: 'Don't kill!'

The second chief component of Hare's account is that ethical judgments, unlike other kinds of command, are 'universalizable'. If I issue a moral injunction, I am thereby committed to holding that that injunction should be obeyed by anyone (including myself) in relevantly similar circumstances. Moral disagreement, the prescriptivist proposes, is a kind of logical impasse, analogous to a situation in which conflicting commands are given; inconsistency and indecision are explained by there being several injunctions, not all of which can be simultaneously obeyed. In this way prescriptivism apparently allows more space for disagreement and debate than emotivism does. Many still question whether it adequately reflects the full depth and complexity of real moral dialogue.

> **I CANNOT SEE HOW TO REFUTE THE ARGUMENTS FOR THE SUBJECTIVITY OF ETHICAL VALUES, BUT I FIND MYSELF INCAPABLE OF BELIEVING THAT ALL THAT IS WRONG WITH WANTON CRUELTY IS THAT I DON'T LIKE IT.**
>
> Bertrand Russell,
> English philosopher, 1960

The condensed idea
Does morality lie within us?

06 Relativism

Is beauty in the eye of the beholder? Doubtless the most familiar question in the field of aesthetics is whether aesthetic values such as beauty are 'real' – inherent, objective – properties of the things to which they are ascribed. Or are such values, rather, inextricably tied to, or dependent on, the judgments and attitudes of the humans who do the ascribing? The assumption of moral relativism, put simply, is that the second answer is the right one and that what goes for aesthetics goes for ethics too.

To a significant degree, the relativist's proposal is that we treat moral judgments as if they were aesthetic ones. If you say you like oysters and I do not, we agree to differ. In such a case it doesn't make sense to say that one or other of us is right or wrong; and it would seem absurd for me to try to persuade you to stop liking oysters or to criticize you for liking them.

In just the same way, the relativist argues, if a particular social group or community approves of, say, infanticide, it is not something that they can be wrong about – it is morally right for them. And it would not be appropriate for others to criticize them or to try to persuade them to change their minds, because there is no neutral standpoint from which to do so. According to this view, then, no moral truth – no moral principle or belief – is 'really' right or wrong; it can be considered so only from the perspective of a particular culture, society or historical period.

TIMELINE

6th century BC

According to Herodotus, Darius the Great of Persia explores the idea of cultural relativism

5th century BC

The case for moral relativism is made by Protagoras and other Greek sophists

CUSTOM IS KING

One of the obvious attractions of relativism is that it fits in well with the great diversity of moral beliefs that exist today and have existed at different times and places in the past. This point has long been recognized. The Greek historian Herodotus, writing in the fifth century BC, tells the story of a party of Greeks at the court of Darius, king of Persia, who are appalled at the suggestion that they should eat the dead bodies of their fathers; they are then confronted with members of a tribe, the Callatians, who follow just such a practice, only to discover that the Callatians are no less disgusted by the Greek habit of burning their dead. Noting that morality is basically a matter of convention, the historian then quotes with approval the poet Pindar's saying: 'Custom is king of all.'

DISAGREEING ABOUT AGREEING TO DISAGREE

One problem with the relativist's treatment of moral judgments as if they were aesthetic ones is that it seems to rule out disagreement over moral values: there is apparently no point arguing the rights and wrongs of either eating oysters or infanticide. Yet in reality our lives are full of such argument and debate: we often take strong positions on ethical matters, such as abortion and capital punishment, and, both individually and as a society, we often change our minds over time. The out-and-out relativist would have to say not only that different things are right for different people but that the same things are right for the same people at one time but not at another. Can the relativist really live with the conclusion that practices such as enslaving people or burning heretics are wrong now but were right in the past, because earlier cultures deemed them so?

Proponents of relativism sometimes attempt to turn its failure to take serious account of ordinary aspects of our moral lives to their advantage.

> **WHAT IS MORALITY IN ANY GIVEN TIME OR PLACE? IT IS WHAT THE MAJORITY THEN AND THERE HAPPEN TO LIKE, AND IMMORALITY IS WHAT THEY DISLIKE.**
>
> Alfred North Whitehead, English philosopher, 1941

1960s

Relativist ideas fuel the growth of 'anything goes' libertarianism

2005

Cardinal Joseph Ratzinger decries the 'dictatorship of relativism'

The dictatorship of relativism

Ideologically opposed to relativism is absolutism, the view that there are certain moral principles that should never be violated, certain actions that are always wrong. Notably absolutist, for example, are religious moralities, which accordingly appear to be especially threatened by relativist ideas. Speaking in 2005, shortly before he became Pope Benedict XVI, Cardinal Joseph Ratzinger delivered a sermon in which he expressed his fears that the certainty of faith, which 'opens us up to all that is good and gives us the knowledge to judge true from false', was being usurped by relativism – a corrosive belief that any point of view is as good as another and hence that it is impossible to reach absolute truth on any matter. The result, he believed, was 'a dictatorship of relativism' – a tyranny that encouraged a false and anarchic sense of freedom and precipitated a descent into moral, and especially sexual, licentiousness.

Perhaps, they argue, we should not be so judgmental of other cultures; we should be *more* tolerant, open-minded and sensitive to other customs and practices. In short, we should live and let live. But this really won't do. For it is only the allegedly intolerant non-relativist who can logically hold up tolerance and cultural sensitivity as virtues that we should all embrace. From the relativist perspective, of course, tolerance is just another value about which different cultures or societies should agree to disagree.

IF ANYTHING GOES ...

From the common but facile judgment that 'it's all relative', it is sometimes inferred that 'anything goes', and in recent decades this has become the slogan of a kind of libertarianism that has set itself against all kinds of traditional or reactionary forces in society, culture and religion. However, the kind of incoherence that afflicts the tolerant relativist quickly overwhelms these more extreme versions of relativism.

Radical relativism is the view that *all* claims – moral and everything else – are relative. So is the claim that all claims are relative itself relative? Well, it has to be, to avoid self-contradiction; but if it is, it means that my claim that all claims are absolute is true *for me*. So, for instance, relativists cannot say that it is always wrong to criticize the cultural arrangements of other societies, as it may be right *for me* to do so. In general, relativists cannot consistently maintain the validity of their own position.

PALATABLE IN MODERATION

The earliest names associated with moral relativism are the sophists of classical Greece – the travelling philosophers and teachers, such as Thrasymachus and Protagoras, who claimed (according to Plato) that it was due to human convention, not to the facts of nature, that things were good or bad, right or wrong, just or unjust. The inconsistencies of Protagoras' relativism are deftly exposed by the Socrates of the Platonic dialogues, but in fact Protagoras seems to have adopted a moderate position, arguing that there must be *some* rules in place (albeit based on convention) to ensure that society can function tolerably.

Protagoras' position is a recognition that we have to agree on *something*, to have *some* common ground, in order to live together as social beings. This is precisely the common ground that is undermined by radical relativism. But in reality, as anthropology has shown, while there may be innumerable differences in detail, many core values are shared by virtually all cultures, past and present: accepted rules against unlawful killing, for instance, without which social living would be impossible; and rules against promise-breaking, without which cooperation would be impossible. A mild dose of relativism, then, may be a healthy corrective to cultural insularity or bigotry. Heavy doses, however, are toxic, inducing something close to moral nihilism.

The condensed idea
Morality by majority vote?

07 The Ring of Gyges

Gyges, a shepherd in the service of King Candaules of Lydia, was tending his sheep when a sudden earthquake exposed an underground tomb. Climbing down, he found a hollow bronze horse containing a giant corpse, the body naked except for a golden ring, which he took off and kept. A little later he discovered that the ring had the power to make him invisible. Chosen as a messenger to report to the king on the state of his flocks, Gyges entered the palace, where he used the ring's power to seduce the queen and murder the king, taking the throne for himself.

Is what Gyges does wrong? And does that make him a bad person? Most of us would probably say 'yes' to the first question, but we might be a bit more cautious about the second. And that is precisely the point that Glaucon, the character in Plato's *Republic* who tells this story, wishes to make. He argues that people behave morally out of necessity, because it is in their interests to do so, not because they really want to. Being seen to act morally gets us a good reputation among our fellows, and that is the surest route to the good things in life – power, wealth and the rest. But given the opportunity that Gyges is given – to act as we please without fear of being caught and punished – we would all do as he does. Without giving a second's thought to whether it is right or wrong, we would lie, steal and kill in order to further our own interests.

The Ring of Gyges, then, raises one of the most fundamental questions in ethics: the issue of moral motivation. Why be good? Are we humans naturally

TIMELINE

7th century BC	*c.*375 BC	1651
Gyges seizes the throne of Lydia	Plato rejects the idea that morality is socially constructed	Thomas Hobbes's *Leviathan* argues that morality is a matter of social convention

good – good for the sake of being good? Or are we good for essentially selfish reasons? Much of the history of philosophy since Plato can be seen as an attempt to answer these most basic questions.

FROM GLAUCON TO HOBBES

The view argued for by Glaucon is that morality is essentially a matter of convention. It is as if everyone has (tacitly) agreed to play by the rules – to refrain from wrongdoing, to abide by the laws laid down by society – because that is the only way that people, collectively, can preserve themselves. The primary motivation is egoism: people act selfishly, but it so happens that the best way to serve their greatest interest – survival – is to forgo their narrower, personal interests. Morality is a kind of truce, reluctantly made and even more grudgingly observed for fear of the consequences of breaking it.

Some two thousand years later, the English philosopher Thomas Hobbes, writing in the gloomy aftermath of the English Civil War, reaches a strikingly similar conclusion. He, too, assumes that humans are essentially self-interested, concerned only to preserve their own security and to increase their own pleasure. Naturally in a state of conflict and competition, everyone is nevertheless best served by cooperation, for only in this way can they escape a condition of war and a life that is 'solitary, poor, nasty, brutish, and short'. This they achieve by consenting to a tacit social contract in which they cede authority to 'a common Power to keep them all in awe' – the absolute power of the state, symbolically named Leviathan.

Further support for the view that ethics is, in the most basic sense, a social construction – that is, the product of pressures exerted on individuals interacting socially – came two centuries later, when Charles Darwin set forth his theory of evolution by natural selection. Darwin goes to great lengths to demonstrate that the content of human minds (including a moral sense),

1762

Jean-Jacques Rousseau, in *The Social Contract*, suggests that civilization is the cause of human corruption

1840s

Karl Marx, with Friedrich Engels, argues that morality is a function of economic conditions

1871

Charles Darwin maintains, in the *Descent of Man*, that morality can be explained in evolutionary terms

Morality and class struggle

In *The Republic*, before Glaucon's challenge to Socrates, the stage is held by a sophist named Thrasymachus. Sharing Glaucon's view that morality is a matter of social convention, he claims that justice – the central theme of Plato's great work – is no more than obedience to society's laws; and as these are invariably framed by the most powerful political group in its own interest, justice is 'nothing more than the interest of the stronger'. As such, Thrasymachus' account interestingly foreshadows the ideas of the most influential political theorist of the 19th century, Karl Marx. According to his materialist conception of history, all ideas, including morality, are the products of the economic stage that society has reached; and, in particular, 'the ideas of the ruling class are in every epoch the ruling ideas'. Thus in capitalist societies, where free movement of labour and expansion of markets are essential, freedom is the predominant value. Famously, of course, Marx also echoes Rousseau in condemning private property as a chief cause of society's ailments. At the crisis of class struggle, when the oppressed workers rise up and overthrow the bourgeois ruling class, transformation will be achieved as the proletariat seize the means of production and abolish private property.

no less than the form of human bodies, is entirely explicable in terms of our descent from other animals. He assembles a great deal of evidence indicating that cooperative behaviour has evolved naturally among intelligent non-human animals living in stable social groups. The development of human moral behaviour, he argues, can be seen as analogous to such processes.

FROM PLATO TO ROUSSEAU

Opposed to Glaucon's view of moral motivation is Plato himself, who speaks in *The Republic* through the character of Socrates, his intellectual mentor. As is typical of the Greeks generally, Plato does not contest Glaucon's assumption that a person's interests are critical in determining what that person should or should not do. What he rejects, though, is the idea that morality is some kind of social construction. Virtue, or moral excellence, in Plato's view, depends on having a proper balance between the three parts of the soul: reason, emotions and appetites. The virtuous man – one whose soul is in harmony – has rational control over earthly ambitions and passions, and so lives at peace with himself, doing good to himself and others. Those like Gyges, on the other hand, who act wrongly, do harm to themselves and others, as they are thereby enslaved to their appetites and live with a soul in discord.

Of all subsequent thinkers, none could be further removed from the bleak outlook of Glaucon or Hobbes than the Genevan Jean-Jacques Rousseau. Whereas Hobbes's pre-social humans, in a 'state of nature', are imagined as living in a condition of ceaseless war 'of every man against every man', Rousseau's state of nature is a rural idyll of 'noble savages' who live together in peace, showing instinctive compassion to their fellows. Contented in 'the sleep of reason', they draw on nature's bounty to satisfy their simple needs. It is only when individuals lay claim to land and the concept of property is born that corruption sets in, leading to the emergence of restrictive customs and laws. It is civilization itself and all its corrupting influences that bring about the loss of innocence. In spite of his uplifting vision, Rousseau himself was under no illusion that a return to some former idyllic condition was possible: once innocence had been lost, he understood that the kind of social constraints envisaged by Hobbes were bound to follow.

The condensed idea
Why be good?

08 Moral intuitions

Common or shared intuitions play a prominent role in moral philosophy. Our intuitive responses to ethical issues and dilemmas are generally taken to be instinctive and immediate, neither having nor needing the support of conscious reasoning. As such they are often thought to offer a special and direct insight into what is right and wrong – a pre-philosophical understanding that must be given serious consideration in the business of moral theorizing.

One reason why moral philosophers tend to be so respectful of our intuitions is a concern that, if they discard them, they will have little else to work with. It is tempting to see these untutored responses as the raw material of ethics – as the rough stone from which solid theory can be built. Any theory relies, ultimately, on some very basic intuitions about what is right and wrong or what is good. So, if we jettison our intuitions, what are we left with beyond a general moral scepticism?

We often assume that our moral intuitions are innate or genetically determined, somehow 'built into' our nature as human beings. Or perhaps we see them as culturally formed – the products, we may suppose, of evolutionary forces acting on social animals interacting with one another over countless generations. Given the significance attached to moral intuitions, it is important to understand them better – to be critical of the way they are used, and to question the basis of their authority and hence their reliability.

TIMELINE

1967, 1976	2000
The trolley problem is first posed by Philippa Foot and later elaborated by Judith Thomson	Jonathan Haidt and team conduct research into the way in which people form moral judgments

INTUITIONS IN THE CAUSE OF THEORY

Moral philosophers tend to invoke common intuitions both in support of their own views and in order to undermine those of others. A close match between a proposed principle or theory and some widely shared intuition is held to be valuable corroboration of that principle or theory; while a standard strategy used in arguing against a given ethical theory is to demonstrate that, in certain circumstances, it may lead to conclusions that run counter to common intuitions. For instance, a utilitarian analysis may suggest that it is sometimes morally justified to sacrifice one or a few innocent lives to save many. The fact that our immediate response to such cases – our instinctive 'gut reaction' – may suggest otherwise is regarded by opponents as significant grounds for rejecting the theory.

Our intuitions about moral issues often conflict, and this, too, is seen by theorists as cause for concern. For example, in the much-discussed set of trolley problems (*see page 61*), the same 'body count' – five lives saved at the cost of one lost – is achieved either by diverting the tram onto a side track or by pushing the fat man off the footbridge. Our intuitions differ, however, suggesting that the former is permissible but not the latter. Theorists therefore set about looking for relevant differences, suggesting, for instance, that in one case (diverting the tram), the harm done is merely foreseen, not intended, and claiming that this difference explains and justifies our differing intuitive responses. The responses themselves, however, are generally assumed to be correct and left unquestioned.

EMOTIONAL AND RATIONAL INTUITIONS

Recent research conducted in the USA has suggested that uncritical confidence in our intuitive responses to ethical situations may be misplaced. Joshua Greene, a researcher at Princeton University, carried out a series of experiments using brain-imaging equipment to investigate the physiological

2001

Joshua Greene and colleagues present the results of their investigation into emotional engagement in moral judgment

2005

Peter Singer proposes that we reconsider the role that intuitions play in ethics

The incest taboo

In order to find out how people reach moral judgments, the psychologist Jonathan Haidt asked people for their response to the following story:

Julie and Mark are brother and sister. They are travelling together in France on summer vacation from college. One night they are staying alone in a cabin near the beach. They decide that it would be interesting and fun if they tried making love. At the very least it would be a new experience for each of them. Julie was already taking birth-control pills, but Mark uses a condom too, just to be safe. They both enjoy making love but decide not to do it again. They keep that night as a special secret between them, which makes them feel even closer to each other. What do you think about that? Was it OK for them to make love?

Almost all the respondents were quick to say that what the siblings did was wrong. When asked to give their reasons, they offered the familiar ones – the danger of inbreeding, the possible psychological damage to the siblings – even though these did not in fact apply in this case. From this it seems clear that the moral verdict the respondents reached was a snap judgment, based on their intuitive response, not on any of the professed reasons. These reasons appear to be a rationalization of their intuition, rather than the basis of it. Tellingly, they were generally unwilling to modify their judgment even after they were obliged to withdraw the reasons that were alleged to support it.

changes that occur in the brain when volunteers are confronted with ethical dilemmas such as the trolley problems. He found that, in cases such as the fat man variant, where the imagined act (pushing the fat man off the bridge) is relatively personal and 'hands-on', the areas of the brain associated with emotions show heightened activity. In contrast, in dilemmas such as the original trolley case, where the act envisaged is relatively impersonal and 'hands-off' (pulling a lever to divert the tram), the parts of the brain concerned with rational (cognitive) activity were more excited.

Greene concluded that we respond differently, at an emotional level, to the idea of pushing someone to their death with our bare hands and bringing about the same result by a more distant or detached means. The former elicits an immediate and strong negative emotional response ('this is wrong!'), the latter a less visceral, more reasoned response ('I should do whatever minimizes harm'). This interpretation is supported by the further observation that the minority of volunteers who thought it right to push the fat man off the bridge took longer to reach their judgment, as if rationalizing and finally overcoming an initial aversion to doing such a thing.

UNTRUSTWORTHY GUIDES?

Partly on the basis of Greene's work, the Australian philosopher Peter Singer – a leading utilitarian – argues that we need to reappraise the role of moral intuitions in ethics. Some of our intuitions, it seems, are essentially emotional, non-rational responses – a fact that is explicable in terms of our evolutionary

> **THE MORAL CONVICTIONS OF THOUGHTFUL AND WELL-EDUCATED PEOPLE ARE THE DATA OF ETHICS JUST AS SENSE-PERCEPTIONS ARE THE DATA OF NATURAL SCIENCE.**
>
> Sir David Ross,
> *The Right and the Good*, 1930

and cultural history but which means that they have no particular authority to guide us in ethical matters. While acknowledging the difficulty of the task, Singer recommends that we should attempt to discriminate between our different intuitive responses, trusting only in those that are rationally based. A useful step, at any rate, would be a greater awareness of the limitations of our moral intuitions and a greater willingness to question their reliability.

The condensed idea
Intuitions – the raw material of ethics?

09 The golden rule

The ethical principle known as the golden rule is captured in the familiar saying 'Do unto others as you would have them do unto you.' Although the name itself seems not to have been used before the 18th century, the underlying idea – or rather group of ideas – is very ancient. It appears, in some guise or other, in almost every ethical code or system, both religious and secular, and is therefore presumed to appeal to one of our most fundamental moral intuitions or instincts.

The golden rule is often associated with Christianity in particular. Sometimes cited as the sum of Jesus' ethics, it features in the Sermon on the Mount and is linked with several central aspects of Christian teaching, such as the commandment to love one's enemies and to love one's neighbour as oneself. However, the rule is also prominent in Jewish and Islamic writings, while variants of it occur in ancient Greek and Roman texts and in the teachings of eastern sages such as Confucius.

A large part of the golden rule's attraction lies in its sheer generality, which explains why it has been so widely and variously interpreted and applied. According to particular taste and need, its dominant facets have been taken to include reciprocity, impartiality and universality. At the same time, the rule's simplicity has exposed it to the criticism that little in the way of substantial practical guidance can be gained from adopting it.

TIMELINE

c.1550–1200 BC	c.500 BC	c.AD 30	1706
Mycenaean civilization coheres around an ethic of reciprocity	Confucius' ethical thinking is founded on the ideas of reciprocity and the golden rule	Jesus' Sermon on the Mount gives a central place to the golden rule	Samuel Clarke elaborates the golden rule in his principle of equity

YOU SCRATCH MY BACK ...

One reason for the golden rule's deep-seated appeal is its endorsement of the ethic of reciprocity. The great importance of returning a favour or benefit received, found in virtually all human societies, has often led to the obligation becoming ritualized. Among the Mycenaean Greeks of the Homeric world, for instance, the giving and receiving of gifts was an essential element in the hospitality rituals that tied bonds of friendship and loyalty and so fostered social cohesion. The Chinese sage Confucius, asked to give a single word that would serve as a guide throughout one's life, is supposed to have replied, 'Surely reciprocity is such a word? What you do not wish to be done to yourself, do not do to others.'

> **AS YOU YOURSELF DESIRE STANDING, THEN HELP OTHERS ACHIEVE IT; AS YOU YOURSELF DESIRE SUCCESS, THEN HELP OTHERS ATTAIN IT.**
> Confucius, c.500 BC

The reasons for reciprocity becoming a near-universal norm are easy to guess. Scratching your own back is more awkward and less effective than getting someone else to do it for you, so entering into a reciprocal arrangement leaves both parties better off. The danger, of course, is that the initial scratchee cheats, seeking a short-term advantage by reneging on the deal. Building an ethic of reciprocity, backed up by social sanctions against non-reciprocators, is intended to discourage such selfish behaviour. Such an ethic is encapsulated by the golden rule.

IMPARTIALITY AND CONSISTENCY

The idea that you should treat others as you wish to be treated might suggest that you should give equal weight to their wishes or interests and hence that you should behave with impartiality towards them. But this is in fact more than the golden rule formally requires. The rule does not demand that you do

Philosophers on the golden rule

The golden rule's appeal is so general that it is easy to find signs of it, more or less explicit, in the works of most moral philosophers. A clear example is the English intuitionist Samuel Clarke, who elaborated the rule in his 'principle of equity': 'Whatever I judge reasonable or unreasonable for another to do for me, that by the same judgment I declare reasonable or unreasonable that I in the like case should do for him.' Kant declared that the golden rule was too trivial to qualify as a universal law, yet its imprint is clear to see in the fundamental principle – the so-called categorical imperative – that underlies his ethical system: 'Act only in accordance with a maxim that you can at the same time will to become a universal law.' The Victorian utilitarian philosopher John Stuart Mill claimed the golden rule for utilitarianism, stating that 'In the golden rule of Jesus of Nazareth, we read the complete spirit of the ethics of utility.' A recent example is the prescriptivist R. M. Hare, whose notion of universalizability, which requires that any moral judgment must be applied impartially to all relevantly similar cases, is an elaboration of the golden rule.

unto others as *they* want to be done by, merely that you treat others as *you* want to be treated, so they will only be treated as they wish if they happen to share your wishes. The most that seems to be required here is that you show consistency in your behaviour, not impartiality. An egoist who wishes to pursue his own self-interest follows the rule and acts consistently in recommending that others do likewise; the masochist who wishes others to inflict pain on him follows the rule and acts consistently in inflicting pain on others – whether they like it or not. The golden rule, on its own, does not necessarily produce substantive moral conclusions.

> **SO IN EVERYTHING, DO UNTO OTHERS AS YOU WOULD HAVE THEM DO UNTO YOU, FOR THIS SUMS UP THE LAW AND THE PROPHETS.**
> Jesus, Sermon on the Mount, C.AD 30

It is this aspect of the golden rule – the prompt towards consistency – that explains why we find hypocrisy obnoxious. The mismatch between what people do and what they recommend others should do –

people not practising what they preach, such as the adulterous politician who pontificates on 'family values' – is objectionable because it is (among other things) inconsistent.

TARNISHED GOLD

The golden rule, then, is no moral panacea. Its very vagueness has allowed people to read into it what they wish to find and to make weighty claims for it that it can scarcely bear. More rule of thumb than golden rule, it nevertheless has a place in the foundations of our ethical thinking: a useful antidote, at least, to the kind of moral myopia that often afflicts people when their own close interests are at stake.

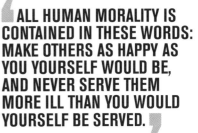

ALL HUMAN MORALITY IS CONTAINED IN THESE WORDS: MAKE OTHERS AS HAPPY AS YOU YOURSELF WOULD BE, AND NEVER SERVE THEM MORE ILL THAN YOU WOULD YOURSELF BE SERVED.

Marquis de Sade, French libertine, 1782

The condensed idea
Do as you would be done by

10 The harm principle

In 1776 the US Declaration of Independence enshrined liberty, alongside life and the pursuit of happiness, in a trinity of natural and inalienable rights endowed upon all humans equally. 'Give me liberty or give me death!' the American revolutionary Patrick Henry had declared a year earlier. Since that time liberty, or freedom, has been widely held to be the most basic of human rights: an ideal worth fighting for and, if need be, dying for; its inestimable value a measure of the many bitter struggles that have been fought to win it.

It might appear to follow from liberty's hallowed status that it should not be qualified or limited in any way. Yet it only takes a moment's thought to see that liberty can never be unlimited or absolute. As the English historian R. H. Tawney observed, 'Freedom for the pike is death for the minnows.' By exercising my freedom to sing loudly in the bath, I deny you the freedom to enjoy a quiet evening. No one can enjoy unfettered freedom – or licence – without encroaching on the freedom of others. The question, then, is how and where we should draw the line.

From a liberal perspective, the standard response to this question is given in the so-called harm (or liberty) principle, which stipulates that individuals should be left free by society to act in any way that does not damage the interests of others. This idea appears in the *Declaration of the Rights of Man and of the Citizen*, the document that boldly affirmed the 'natural and imprescriptible rights of man' at the outset of the French Revolution in 1789:

> Liberty consists in the freedom to do everything which injures no one else; hence the exercise of the natural rights of each man has no limits except those which assure to the other members of the society the enjoyment of the same rights.

The principle is best known, however, in the form set forth in *On Liberty* (1859) by the Victorian philosopher John Stuart Mill:

> The only purpose for which power can be rightfully exercised over any member of a civilised community, against his will, is to prevent harm to others. His own good, either physical or moral, is not a sufficient warrant.

BERLIN AND NEGATIVE FREEDOM

The form of liberty created by application of the harm principle is the kind later characterized by the philosopher Isaiah Berlin, in his famous essay *Two Concepts of Liberty* (1958), as 'negative freedom'. Such liberty is negative in that it is defined by what is absent – any form of external constraint or coercion; you are free in this sense as long as there is no obstacle preventing you from doing what you wish to do.

> **WHAT FREEDOM MEANS IS BEING ALLOWED TO SING IN MY BATH AS LOUDLY AS WILL NOT INTERFERE WITH MY NEIGHBOUR'S FREEDOM TO SING A DIFFERENT TUNE IN HIS.**
>
> Tom Stoppard,
> British playwright, 2002

Berlin's view is that there should be an area of private liberty that is sacrosanct and immune to outside interference and authority, a space where a person is 'left to do or be what he is able to do or be'. It is within this space that individuals should be allowed to indulge their personal tastes and inclinations without hindrance,

1859

John Stuart Mill's *On Liberty* gives the classic account of the harm principle

1958

Isaiah Berlin's *Two Concepts of Liberty* defines negative and positive liberty

2001

George W. Bush declares a war on terror

provided that their doing so does not harm others or prevent them from enjoying a similar freedom. Thus the harm principle is intimately linked to another great pillar of liberalism – toleration.

FROM PATERNALISM TO TYRANNY

Critics of the harm principle may focus on the practical inadequacy of the liberty it protects. It is true, perhaps, that any citizen of the USA is free (in the negative sense) to become president – there is no legal or constitutional bar to their doing so; but are they *truly* free if lack of the necessary resources, in terms of money, social status, education or character, renders such an event a practical impossibility? In such cases, people appear to lack the substantive freedom to exercise the rights that they formally hold. What is lacking here is what Berlin calls 'positive freedom' – not merely *freedom from* outside interference but an active *freedom to* achieve certain ends: a form of empowerment that allows individuals to fulfil their potential, to realize their dreams, to act autonomously and control their destiny.

THOSE WHO HAVE EVER VALUED LIBERTY FOR ITS OWN SAKE BELIEVED THAT TO BE FREE TO CHOOSE, AND NOT TO BE CHOSEN FOR, IS AN INALIENABLE INGREDIENT IN WHAT MAKES HUMAN BEINGS HUMAN

Isaiah Berlin,
Five Essays on Liberty, 1969

For those, including Berlin, who support the harm principle, the case for it is built in part on observing what emerges when it is not applied – a kind of paternalism in which people take it upon themselves to promote (what they assume to be) positive freedom in the lives of others. Perhaps setting out with perfectly good intentions, people are quick to conclude that there is a right path that others would readily follow if only they knew better – if only their 'better side' prevailed, or maybe if their worse side were suppressed. From there it is a short step, as Berlin ruefully observes, for those in authority to assume the right 'to ignore the actual wishes of men or societies, to bully, oppress, torture in the name, and on behalf, of [people's] "real" selves'.

In extreme cases, what starts out as social reform may be transformed into zealotry, justifying, it seems, the kind of tyranny that insists on conformity

Liberty sacrificed on the altar of security

So what kinds of harm give sufficient grounds for curtailing liberty? One of the most controversial is the threat to national security. The radical Thomas Paine wrote in 1795, 'he that would make his own liberty secure must guard even his enemy from oppression', but few since have taken much notice of his words. The French revolutionaries' excuse for sweeping aside civil liberties was the threat of counter-revolution at home and the menace of foreign armies abroad. Sadly, subsequent governments, despite their claims to love liberty, have tended to copy the French model, forgetting the warning of fourth US president, James Madison: 'The means of defence against foreign danger historically have become the instruments of tyranny at home.' In September 2001, in the wake of the 9/11 Islamist attacks, a later president, George W. Bush, declared a war on terror – 'civilization's fight ... the fight of all who believe in progress and pluralism, tolerance and freedom'. The war was supposed to usher in 'an age of liberty', but over the following years its casualties included many civil liberties and human rights.

in pursuit of a society's goals and dehumanizes its citizens in the process. Tellingly, Berlin's own deep distrust of positive freedom was fuelled in large part by the enormities of the 20th century, especially the totalitarian horrors of Stalin's Soviet Union. 'All forms of tampering with human beings,' Berlin concludes, 'getting at them, shaping them against their will to your own pattern, all thought control and conditioning is, therefore, a denial of that in men which makes them men and their values ultimate.'

The condensed idea
Setting the limits of liberty

11 Ends and means

A Gestapo officer rounds up five children and threatens to kill them unless you name and shoot a fugitive spy. As it happens, you didn't know that there was a spy, let alone his or her identity, but you are quite certain both that the officer won't believe you if you plead ignorance and that he will carry out his threat. So: do you tell the truth and let five innocent children die? Or do you tell a lie, naming and killing an innocent person to save the five?

People take different views on dilemmas such as this. A few (perhaps mainly moral theorists) think that it is always wrong to lie, so you should tell the truth in such circumstances, even though the officer won't believe you and five children will be killed. Others feel that it matters a lot that it is you who is doing the shooting: it is an absolute duty not to kill people, so you should refuse to do so, come what may. Others still think that it is simply wrong to do something (*actively* do something, that is) that you know will cause the death of an innocent person – it is simply too high a price to pay. What these various approaches have in common is that they all give priority to some notion of duty: the idea that there are certain kinds of things, such as telling the truth, that we should do simply because it is the right thing to do; and certain kinds of things, such as lying, that we should avoid doing because they are plain wrong.

In contrast, there are other moral theorists (as well as ordinary people) who do not think that our actions and decisions are right or wrong in themselves.

TIMELINE

*c.*350 BC	1785	late 18th century
Aristotle's ethics focuses on the character of the moral agent	Immanuel Kant analyses duty in *Groundwork of the Metaphysics of Morals*	Jeremy Bentham lays the foundations of classical utilitarianism

Peeping Tom

Tom gets his kicks by spying on a woman through her bedroom window, secretly taking pictures of her as she gets undressed. He's never caught, she never finds out, and he only uses the photos for his own pleasure. If you only consider the consequences of what Tom does, it seems that his actions lead to a net gain in overall well-being (his pleasure is enhanced and nobody else is affected) and hence – for the consequentialist – they should be regarded as morally acceptable. Most people's gut tells them otherwise, however. In indulging his voyeuristic urges, Tom infringes the woman's rights – in particular, her right to privacy. The whole point of rights is to restrict the ways in which people can be (mis)treated, and any supposedly desirable consequences that result from flouting them are beside the point. In the matter of rights, therefore, a duty-based understanding of morality seems to sit more comfortably with our common intuitions than a consequentialist approach.

It is the different outcomes of what we decide to do that really matter. So, in order to assess whether an action is right or wrong, we do not need to consider what *type* of action is being performed; rather, we should look at the consequences that it brings about. In the Gestapo case, one course of action leads to the death of five innocent children, the other to the death of one innocent person. Other things being equal, one death is better than five, so the right thing to do is to sacrifice the one to save the many.

DO ENDS JUSTIFY MEANS?

One way of highlighting the contrast between these different approaches is in terms of ends and means. For one who looks at the consequences of an action to determine whether it is right or wrong – a consequentialist – an action has only instrumental value, as a means to some desirable end; its

1861

John Stuart Mill's essay
Utilitarianism defends and
elaborates Bentham's theory

1958

Modern virtue ethics is
developed by Elizabeth
Anscombe and others

Thought experiments

Moral philosophers often use thought experiments, like the Gestapo story or the Peeping Tom case, because an imagined scenario can (so it is hoped) exclude irrelevant details and hence isolate the particular responses or intuitions elicited by principles or other ideas under review. However, the implications of such experiments can readily be applied to real-world situations, including matters of life and death. In real life, people sometimes find themselves in situations where it is necessary to prioritize some lives over others. Politicians, for instance, are obliged to make decisions that cause (or contribute to, or fail to prevent) the deaths of innocent people – decisions about the use of public money and priorities in the health service, about the use of military forces, about the allocation of social welfare resources. Different approaches to such issues are determined by all sorts of influences (cultural, religious, philosophical among others) and are likely to result in very different decisions and hence outcomes – outcomes in which some people are, in effect, allowed to live and others condemned to die.

rightness or wrongness is a measure of how effective it is in achieving that end. It is the end itself – some state of affairs, a condition of general well-being or happiness, for example – that really matters. So, in choosing between various available courses of action, the consequentialist will weigh up the good and bad outcomes in each case and reach a decision on that basis.

THE END MAY JUSTIFY THE MEANS SO LONG AS THERE IS SOMETHING THAT JUSTIFIES THE END.
Leon Trotsky, Marxist revolutionary and theorist, 1936

By contrast, in a duty-based system, actions are not seen merely as means to an end but as right or wrong in themselves; they have intrinsic value, not just instrumental value in contributing towards some desirable end. Someone looking at a moral issue from such a perspective may consider that killing, say, is intrinsically wrong and cannot be justified by any good consequences that are claimed to flow from it.

DUTY VERSUS CONSEQUENCES

The separation of ethical systems into those based on duty (deontological) and those based on consequences (consequentialist) is too simple. For one thing, even within the limits of the Western philosophical tradition, there are other approaches that do not see morality in terms of right and wrong action at all, but focus instead on the character of moral agents, asking not what kind of things we should do but what kind of people we should be. Such an approach goes back to Aristotle and has been revived over the past century in the guise of contemporary virtue ethics (*see chapter 20*).

Be that as it may, for most of the past 400 years moral philosophers have seen it as their primary task to discover and explain the principles and rules that inform and guide (or should inform and guide) our behaviour. And in this task the chief polarities of the debate have been duty and consequences, with the deontological system of Immanuel Kant leading the way at one end and the consequentialist utilitarianism of Jeremy Bentham and John Stuart Mill at the other (*see chapters 12 and 13*).

The condensed idea
The ethics of duty and consequences

12 Utilitarianism

A transplant surgeon finds herself in the distressing position of having four patients, all of whom are about to die through want of suitable organs (a liver, a heart and two kidneys). By chance a healthy student, on a work placement with the surgeon, happens to be a perfect donor for all the required organs. The surgeon sedates the student, removes the organs, and carries out the transplant operations, thereby saving the four patients.

Many of today's philosophers argue that morality should be based on consequentialist grounds: the question of whether our actions are right or wrong should be decided by considering the consequences of those actions. Utilitarianism, the most influential of consequentialist theories, is the more specific view that actions should be judged right or wrong to the extent that they increase or decrease general well-being or 'utility'.

On the face of it, the transplant scenario looks as if it results in a net gain in human well-being. Assuming that all the parties concerned are equally content with life, have similar prospects for happiness, and so on, four valuable lives have apparently been preserved at the cost of one such life. So, on utilitarian grounds, it appears that the surgeon has done the right thing. Yet almost everybody would agree that her behaviour is indefensible. On the face of it, an ethical theory that produces conclusions that run counter to virtually everyone's intuitions looks like a bad theory. So what exactly is utilitarianism and how does it cope with scenarios like this?

TIMELINE

18th century	1861
Jeremy Bentham lays the foundations of classical utilitarianism	John Stuart Mill's essay *Utilitarianism* defends and elaborates Bentham's theory

CLASSICAL UTILITARIANISM

The roots of utilitarianism go back to the work of the radical philosopher Jeremy Bentham in the late 18th century. For him, utility lay solely in human pleasure or happiness, and his theory is sometimes summarized as the promotion of 'the greatest happiness of the greatest number'. One of utilitarianism's chief attractions, in his view, was that it held out the promise of a rational and scientific basis on which policies about the legal structure and organization of society could be founded. To this end, he proposed a 'felicific calculus', according to which the different amounts of pleasure and pain produced by different actions could be measured and compared; the right action on a given occasion could then be determined by a (supposedly) simple process of addition and subtraction.

'BETTER TO BE SOCRATES DISSATISFIED'

Critics were quick to point out just how narrow a conception of morality Bentham had given. By supposing that life had no higher end than pleasure, he had apparently left out of the reckoning all sorts of things that we would normally count as inherently valuable, such as knowledge, love, honour, achievement and life itself. As his younger contemporary and fellow utilitarian John Stuart Mill put it, Bentham had produced 'a doctrine worthy only of swine'.

Mill was troubled by this criticism and sought to modify utilitarianism accordingly. While Bentham had allowed only two variables in measuring pleasure – duration and intensity – Mill introduced a third, quality, thereby creating a hierarchy of 'higher and lower pleasures'.

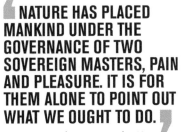

NATURE HAS PLACED MANKIND UNDER THE GOVERNANCE OF TWO SOVEREIGN MASTERS, PAIN AND PLEASURE. IT IS FOR THEM ALONE TO POINT OUT WHAT WE OUGHT TO DO.

Jeremy Bentham, *Introduction to the Principles of Morals and Legislation*, 1789

According to this distinction, some pleasures, such as those of the intellect and the arts, are by their nature more valuable than base physical ones, and

1970s

Peter Singer and others propose that satisfaction of desires or preferences is the proper measure of utility

1974

Robert Nozick's experience machine threatens the claim that pleasure alone is intrinsically good

The experience machine

Imagine an 'experience machine' that simulates a life in which all your fondest dreams and ambitions are realized. Once plugged into the machine, you will have no idea that you are plugged in and you will think that everything is real. 'Would you plug in?' asks the US philosopher Robert Nozick: would you exchange a real life of inevitable frustration and disappointment for a virtual existence of unalloyed pleasure and success? In spite of its obvious attractions, most people, Nozick supposes, would reject the offer. The reality of life, its *authenticity*, is important to us: we want to do certain things, not just experience the pleasure of doing them. Yet, if pleasure were the only thing that mattered, surely we would all gladly plug in. So there must be things apart from pleasure that we consider intrinsically valuable. But if this is so, then something must be wrong with utilitarianism, at least in its classical hedonistic (pleasure-based) formulation.

by giving them greater weight in the calculus of pleasure, Mill was able to conclude that it was 'better to be a human being dissatisfied than a pig satisfied; better to be Socrates dissatisfied than a fool satisfied'.

THE COST OF COMPLEXITY

Mill's introduction of a complex concept of pleasure was made at some cost. His notion of different kinds of pleasure seems to require some criterion other than pleasure to tell them apart. If something other than pleasure is a constituent of Mill's idea of utility, it is questionable whether his theory remains strictly utilitarian at all.

Getting a more intuitive answer to the case of the transplant surgeon also requires some special pleading. A classical utilitarian might argue, perhaps, that sacrificing one student to save four patients actually represents a net *loss* of utility: the erosion of trust between patients and doctors caused by the latter habitually behaving in such a manner would cause more harm than good in the long run. But in the end, utilitarians have to bite the bullet and admit that, if it is clear that none of these bad things will happen and there will indeed be a net gain in utility, the surgeon should go ahead and carve up the student.

ACT AND RULE UTILITARIANS

These difficulties are reflected in a significant split that has occurred in Bentham and Mill's theory concerning the precise manner in which the utilitarian standard is to be applied to actions. So-called 'act' utilitarians require that each action is assessed directly in terms of its individual contribution to utility; 'rule' utilitarians, on the other hand, determine an appropriate course of action by reference to various sets of rules that will, if generally followed, promote utility. For instance, killing innocent people as a *rule* decreases utility, even though it might appear to have beneficial short-term consequences, so carving up the student turns out to be wrong after all.

Applying rules in this way also helps to overcome the objection that utilitarianism is simply not practicable. If we have to do a precise auditing of the utility that results from every possible course of action before we do anything, we will usually end up doing nothing – and that won't generally be the right thing to do. But if we apply principles that are known, as a rule, to promote general well-being, we will usually do the right thing. We may know from past experience that overall utility is diminished by lying and stealing, for instance, and therefore that we should not lie or steal.

Rules may seem to be useful in such cases, but what if it is obvious that breaking a rule will increase overall well-being? What if telling a white lie, for instance, will clearly save innocent lives? None of the options available to the rule utilitarian is very attractive. She can stick to the rule about lying and knowingly bring about bad consequences; or she can break the rule and undermine her status as a rule utilitarian. The only other option, it seems, is to modify the rule in this case, but rules, adapted to suit a particular situation, are not really rules at all. They are bound to become increasingly complex and qualified, to the point where a rule-based system collapses into an act-based one.

Utilitarianism remains a highly influential approach to ethics. Many philosophers, attracted by its foursquare merits, continue to chisel away at it, ever hopeful of smoothing out its rougher edges. It is fair to say, however, that these edges stubbornly remain, and its many critics continue to suggest that the whole venture was misguided from the outset.

The condensed idea
The greatest happiness principle

13 Kantian ethics

You are sheltering a political dissident whom the repressive ruling regime has vowed to hunt down and execute. The secret police bang on your door and ask if you know the whereabouts of the dissident. You are in no doubt that if you tell them, your charge will be arrested and shot. What should you do? Tell the truth or tell a lie?

The question hardly seems worth asking. Of course you should lie – a very white lie, you may think, given the terrible consequences of telling the truth. But it has not seemed so simple to all moral theorists, at least not to the 18th-century German theorist Immanuel Kant, one of the most influential philosophers of the past 300 years. In his view, telling the truth is a duty that is absolute and unconditional: lying contravenes a fundamental principle of morality – what he calls a 'categorical imperative'.

HYPOTHETICAL AND CATEGORICAL IMPERATIVES

Kant explains what a categorical imperative is, first, by contrasting it with a *hypothetical* imperative – a non-moral prompting to which you should respond if you wish to achieve some further end. Suppose I tell you what to do by issuing an order (an imperative): 'Stop smoking!' Implicitly, there is a string of conditions that I might attach to this command – 'if you don't want to risk your health', for instance, or 'if you don't want to waste your money'. Of course, if you don't care about your health or your money, the order carries no weight and you need not comply.

TIMELINE

4th–13th century BC	1775–83
God delivers Ten Commandments to Moses on Mount Sinai	System of rights and duties is established in the USA by the American Revolution

Moral dilemmas

The question of whether lying is morally unacceptable, whatever the consequences, was put to Kant in his lifetime, and he unfalteringly stuck by his categorical guns, insisting that it is indeed one's moral duty to be truthful on all occasions, even to a murderer. But in fact the situation is not as simple as it seems. For is it not inevitable that categorical imperatives will clash? 'Help innocent people avoid arbitrary execution' looks like a good candidate as a categorical imperative: we could surely will this to be a universal maxim. And if it is a moral law, it clashes – in the case of our fictional political dissident – with the absolute duty not to lie. We are in a moral dilemma in which we have no choice but to violate one or other of what appear to be categorical imperatives. Disquiet with an ethical system that apparently results in duties that are both absolute and contradictory has encouraged some to take a more flexible, less absolutist approach towards the notion of duty (*see chapter 14*).

In the case of a categorical imperative, by contrast, there are no ifs attached, implicit or otherwise. 'Don't lie!' and 'Don't kill people!' are injunctions that are not hypothesized on any aim or desire that you may or may not have; they must be followed as a matter of duty, unconditionally and without exception. Indeed, according to Kant, it is only actions performed purely from a sense of duty that have moral worth. Actions prompted by some external motivation – a desire to help a friend, for instance, or to achieve a particular goal – are not distinctively moral actions at all. In contrast to hypothetical imperatives, categorical imperatives constitute moral laws.

UNIVERSAL MAXIMS

Kant believes that beneath every action there is an underlying rule of conduct, or maxim. Such maxims may have the *form* of categorical imperatives, but they do not qualify as moral laws unless they pass the test of universality,

1785

Immanuel Kant analyses duty in
*Groundwork of the Metaphysics
of Morals*

1847

Benjamin Disraeli's novel
Tancred is published

God-given duty

Kant's system of absolute duties may be the most influential of such *philosophical* theories, but for the most important influence in this area we must look elsewhere. 'Duty cannot exist without faith,' wrote Benjamin Disraeli in 1847. For most of humanity, for most of its history, the ultimate authority for the responsibilities or obligations that we call duties has been divine and hence absolute. Usually passed down through scripture and mediated by priesthood, the wishes and commands of a god or gods impose obligations on humans, whose duty it is to meet these obligations, by adopting certain codes of conduct, for instance, and performing various services and sacrifices in honour of the deity/deities. In the Judaeo-Christian tradition, the most familiar example is the Ten Commandments, a set of divine prescriptions that impose a number of absolute duties on mankind: a duty not to kill, another not to covet your neighbour's wife, and so on.

which is itself a supreme form of categorical imperative:

> Act only in accordance with a maxim that you can at the same time will to become a universal law.

This test ensures that an action is morally permissible only if it accords with a rule that you can consistently and universally apply to yourself and others. For instance, to test whether lying qualifies as a universal law, we might suppose some such maxim as 'Lie whenever you feel like it.' What happens when this principle is universalized? Well, lying is possible only in a context in which the general expectation is that people are telling the truth. But if *everyone* lied all the time, nobody would trust anybody else, and lying would be impossible. The idea of lying as a universal law is thus incoherent and self-defeating. Likewise, stealing presupposes a culture of property ownership, but the whole concept of property would collapse if *everybody* stole; breaking promises presupposes a generally accepted institution of promise-keeping; and so on.

While the requirement of universality rules out certain kinds of conduct on logical grounds, there seem to be many others that we could universalize, yet would not wish to count as moral. 'Always look after your own interests', 'Break promises where you can do so without undermining the institution of promising' – there doesn't appear to be anything inconsistent or irrational in willing that these should become universal laws. So how does Kant head off this danger?

PURE REASON AND AUTONOMY

The genius of Kant's ethical system is how he moves from the purely rational structure imposed by the categorical imperative to actual moral content – to explain how 'pure reason', stripped of inclination or desire, can inform and direct the will of a moral agent. The answer lies in the inherent value of moral agency itself – value based on the 'single supreme principle of morality', the freedom or autonomy of a will that obeys laws that it imposes on itself. The supreme importance attached to autonomous, free-willed agents is mirrored in the second great formulation of the categorical imperative:

> Act in such a way that you always treat humanity, whether in your own person or in the person of any other, never simply as a means, but always at the same time as an end.

> TWO THINGS MOVE THE MIND WITH EVER-INCREASING ADMIRATION AND AWE, THE OFTENER AND MORE STEADILY WE REFLECT ON THEM: THE STARRY HEAVENS ABOVE AND THE MORAL LAW WITHIN.
>
> Immanuel Kant,
> *Critique of Practical Reason*, 1788

Once the incomparable value of one's own moral agency is recognized, it is necessary to extend that respect to the agency of others. Treating others merely as a means to promote one's own interests is to destroy their agency, so maxims that are self-serving or damaging to others contravene this formulation of the categorical imperative and so do not qualify as moral laws. In essence, there is a recognition here that there are basic rights that belong to people by virtue of their humanity and that may not be overridden – and hence that there are duties that must be obeyed, come what may.

The condensed idea
Thou shalt not …
come what may?

14 *Prima facie* duties

Common sense suggests to many that there is more to doing what is right than maximizing happiness (or good), as utilitarians suppose. There should, surely, be a place for duty – the idea that some things are worth doing simply because they are the right things to do. And yet the sheer austerity of Kant's notion of absolute duties, to be followed come what may, seems to take things too far. Our lives are full of moral compromise and dilemma, where numerous claims compete and conflict, dragging us simultaneously in different directions.

I f it really happened that the secret police knocked at my door, intent on shooting my lodger (*see page 52*), I should of *course* lie about her whereabouts. Kant's absolutism seems crazy in this case. And yet the justification for telling such a lie is not, as the utilitarian suggests, that I would thereby bring about a net gain in human happiness (or good). Perhaps I would, perhaps I wouldn't. The simple fact of the matter is that, in these circumstances, my duty to protect an individual is more pressing than my duty to tell the truth.

ROSS ON DUTIES

One of the great attractions of the Scottish philosopher Sir David Ross's view of morality, set forth in the first half of the 20th century, is that it

TIMELINE

1785	late 18th century
Immanuel Kant gives an absolutist account of duty in *Groundwork of the Metaphysics of Morals*	Jeremy Bentham lays the foundations of classical utilitarianism

sits comfortably with common sense, reflecting the perennial human struggle to determine the right thing to do in any given situation and then to do it. He recognizes that we have many moral duties and that these often conflict with one another.

In Ross's view, while we acknowledge numerous such duties, these are not absolutely binding. In considering how we should act, it is our task as moral agents to weigh up the competing claims and to reach a decision that is right in the circumstances. He calls these duties *prima facie*, from the Latin meaning 'on first appearance', not because they are not genuine obligations, but because they can be overridden and may have to yield to other duties that take precedence in a particular situation.

ANY POSSIBLE ACT HAS MANY SIDES TO IT WHICH ARE RELEVANT TO ITS RIGHTNESS OR WRONGNESS.

Sir David Ross,
The Right and the Good, 1930

While stressing that his list is not necessarily complete, Ross enumerates seven kinds of *prima facie* duty:
1 **Fidelity** The duty to be honest (tell the truth, keep promises).
2 **Reparation** The duty to compensate for a previous wrongful act.
3 **Gratitude** The duty to acknowledge services done by others.
4 **Justice** The duty to be fair (to resist unjust distribution of goods).
5 **Beneficence** The duty to help others less fortunate.
6 **Self-improvement** The duty to improve one's own virtue, intelligence, etc.
7 **Non-maleficence** The duty not to harm others.

BALANCING DUTIES
Ross gives a number of examples to show how, in practice, competing *prima facie* duties can be weighed and appraised, through moral reflection, in order to determine an actual duty – that is, what it is in fact right to do in a particular set of circumstances. Considering a conflict between the claims of

1930
Sir David Ross's *The Right and the Good* gives an account of morality in terms of *prima facie* duties

fidelity (keeping a promise) and of beneficence (helping someone in distress), he writes:

> Besides the duty of fulfilling promises I have and recognize a duty of relieving distress, and ... when I think it right to do the latter at the cost of not doing the former, it is not because I think I shall produce more good thereby but because I think it the duty which is in the circumstances more of a duty.

Here, Ross makes it clear that such judgments should not be made (solely) on utilitarian grounds – that is, by adopting whatever course produces more happiness or good. He concedes that bringing about the best possible consequences may be a *prima facie* duty, but it is of course only one of many and not necessarily the most important.

Indeed, elsewhere Ross is explicitly *anti-utilitarian*. He imagines a situation in which keeping a promise to person A produces very slightly less good for her than doing some other act would produce for person B, to whom no promise has been made. He judges that (other things being equal) it is our duty to keep the promise, thereby rejecting the utilitarian response. It is a matter of degree, however, and each case must be considered on its merits. For if breaking the promise produced 'a much greater disparity of value between the total consequences' for A and B, he thinks that (other things being equal) we would be justified in not keeping our word. Ross, clearly, is neither utilitarian nor absolutist.

Helping and harming others

Suppose that it is the rush hour and you are in the Underground, standing at the edge of the platform as the train approaches. Suddenly the crowd behind you surges, threatening to push the person standing next to you onto the tracks and in front of the train. At the last moment, you barge somebody else off the platform and onto the tracks, thereby making room for the person next to you, saving her life. The classic utilitarian response here is that it makes no difference, morally, what you do. However, Ross, as usual, stays closer to our common intuitions, insisting that in such cases the duty of beneficence (helping others) is trumped by the duty of non-maleficence (not harming others): 'We should not in general consider it justifiable to kill one person in order to keep another alive.'

WHERE DO DUTIES COME FROM?

The picture Ross gives of conflicting duties competing for priority seems to mirror the common view of how we reach moral decisions. But how and whence does he derive the *prima facie* duties around which his theory revolves?

Ross believes that 'the convictions of thoughtful, well-educated people' provide 'the data of ethics'. His *prima facie* duties are self-evident, he thinks, to people who reflect clearly and calmly, with minds undistorted by self-interest or faulty moral upbringing. In other words, we have an intuitive grasp of these moral truths, which neither require nor admit of evidence beyond themselves.

The problem with things beyond proof is that they cannot be shown to be right or wrong. We can never be sure that what seems self-evident to Ross will seem so to others; indeed, the fact that other theorists find things self-evident and that these things are not always the same as Ross's suggests that we are justified in being sceptical about such claims. Similar concerns about the fallibility of intuition surround Ross's attempts to explain how and when, in particular situations, one duty is found to be less pressing than another and so should give way to it.

A suspicion lingers that Ross has given a plausible account of how moral deliberation works without encouraging much confidence that the fruits of that deliberation are securely founded.

The condensed idea
Making sense of moral conflict

15 Double effect

'Let justice be done though the heavens fall': absolutist moralities hold that there are certain kinds of action that are *always* wrong, whatever the consequences. Deliberately killing an innocent person, for instance, is intrinsically wrong – wrong in itself – and cannot be justified under any circumstances. Kantian ethics takes this view, as do many varieties of religious morality, in which absolute moral prescriptions are believed to be based on the infallible word of God.

A big problem for absolutism is that there are many circumstances where common sense suggests that we should override its rigid injunctions. If the only way of preventing 'the heavens falling' – or, less figuratively, the loss, say, of millions of innocent lives – were the deliberate sacrifice of one innocent life, would it not be perverse not to make such a sacrifice? Can it really be wrong to kill a foetus to save a woman's life, if the only alternative is that both die? Or for a soldier to deliberately kill himself by throwing himself on a grenade, in order to save his comrades?

Absolutists must either accept that such actions are wrong or find some way of interpreting them that is consistent with their moral views. Historically, the most important approach of this kind, notably within the Catholic tradition, has been the doctrine of double effect. This doctrine or principle attempts to draw a morally significant distinction between the good and bad consequences (whence 'double effect') of an action. It is morally permissible, it is claimed, for an agent to carry out the action if she intends to bring about the good consequences and merely foresees the bad ones. In other words, it may be acceptable to perform a good act in the knowledge that bad consequences will follow, but it is always wrong to carry out a bad act as a means to achieve some good outcome.

THE TROLLEY PROBLEM
To see how the doctrine works, consider the following case:

There is a runaway tram (trolley car) hurtling down the track, heading straight towards five people a little farther down the line. Next to you is a lever, which, if pulled, will divert the tram onto a side track. You notice that there is, unfortunately, one person on the side track. If you do nothing, the five people on the main track will be killed; if you pull the lever, the tram will be diverted, saving the five but killing the person on the side track. What should you do?

Most people feel that you should pull the lever in such a situation. A classic utilitarian analysis would agree with this intuition. Other things being equal, sacrificing one life to save five produces a net gain in utility (happiness). Ross's moderate ethics of *prima facie* duties (*see chapter 14*) might also be in accord with the popular view. He recognizes a strong duty not to harm others and a less urgent duty to help others, but they are not absolute. Is there sufficient benefit in this case to justify overriding the stronger duty? That is a matter for careful moral reflection, but it is at least an open question. It is only the absolutist who seems to be at variance with the common intuition here. If it is always wrong to kill, it is wrong to kill the person on the side track. Period.

This is where the doctrine of double effect comes in. It is your *intention*, the absolutist claims, to save the five people on the main track. In the course

1976

The fat man version of the trolley problem is devised by US philosopher Judith Thomson

1985

Thomson introduces the loop variant of the trolley problem

The looping trolley

A simple modification to the original trolley problem casts doubt on the distinction between intention and foresight on which the doctrine of double effect depends. Suppose the side track (with one person) that branches from the main track (with five people) loops back onto the main track, so if you pull the lever and divert the tram, it will loop around and kill the five people. It is only the presence of the person on the side track that blocks the tram and stops it from looping around and killing the five on the main track. In this case, the death of the person on the side track *is* intended as the means by which the five are saved. Most people think, however, that it is still right to pull the lever. This common intuition, if sound, suggests that the intention/foresight distinction is not the crucial issue in these cases.

of realizing this admirable aim, you foresee, with regret, that the unfortunate person on the side track will die. This death is not part of your intention, however – it is a foreseeable but unintended side effect – so the action in question is morally permissible.

THE FAT MAN ON THE BRIDGE

To see the kind of distinction that the doctrine draws, consider a slightly modified scenario:

As before, the tram is running out of control, heading towards five people farther ahead on the line. But this time you are standing on a bridge over the track, watching events from above. There is a very large man standing next to you. You realize that, if you push him off the bridge and onto the track below, his massive body will get in the way of the tram, stopping it before it can reach the five people on the line. If you do nothing, the five people will be hit by the tram and killed; if you push the fat man off the bridge, he will be killed but the five will be saved. What should you do?

From a strictly utilitarian standpoint, the answer remains the same: the balance of gain – one life lost to save five – is unchanged, so you should go ahead and push the fat man. But the common intuition here is reversed – most people's gut feeling is that it is wrong to deliberately kill someone in these circumstances – and the doctrine of double effect gives a possible explanation. In this case, the death of the fat man is actually required: the harm done to him is not merely foreseen but intended as the means of saving the others, and therefore the action is (according to the doctrine) morally impermissible.

THE DOUBLE EFFECT IN MEDICINE

In the real world, the doctrine of double effect has been most prominent in the area of medical ethics. The usual treatment for cancer of the uterus is removal of the diseased organ (hysterectomy), a procedure that, in the case of a pregnant woman, will cause the certain death of the foetus. This is permitted by the doctrine on the grounds that the foetal death is seen (or foreseen) as an unwanted side effect of the laudable intention of saving the woman's life. On the other hand, craniotomy – a procedure that involves crushing the foetus's skull – is prohibited, because in this case killing the foetus is the direct means used to save the woman's life.

Another oft-cited example is the situation where a doctor prescribes powerful painkillers in the treatment of a terminally ill patient. It is foreseen that such drugs may shorten the patient's life, but their use is considered morally acceptable provided that they are given with the intention of relieving pain. However, to administer drugs *in order* to shorten life and thereby reduce suffering would not be permissible.

DOUBLE TROUBLE

As these real-life examples show, the central problem facing the doctrine of double effect is to make a convincing distinction between what is intended and what is merely foreseen. In particular, there is a concern that an ethical issue can always be characterized in such a way as to accommodate an existing prejudice on the matter. Thus, for instance, what supporters of abortion describe as a hysterectomy will be portrayed by their opponents as an abortion; each side will end up back where they started, with the debate no further advanced. When reduced in this way to the level of semantics, the doctrine of double effect holds little promise of offering insights of real moral substance.

The condensed idea
Intending and foreseeing harm

16 Acts and omissions

It is a commonly held view that there is a significant difference, morally, between what we do and what we allow to happen. It may be very bad not to warn someone if you see a tree falling on her head, but both ethically and legally, it is considered much worse to bring about the same outcome by deliberately sawing the tree down. This distinction underlies the so-called 'acts and omissions doctrine'.

The idea that there is an important moral difference between doing something and allowing something to happen serves a similar purpose, in an ethics based on strict and unconditional duties, to the doctrine of double effect (*see page 60*). The absolutist – religious or other – who embraces the idea of double effect, proposes that bringing about innocent deaths (for instance) as an unintended side effect is not prohibited in the same way as intentional killing. In a similar vein, the proponent of the acts and omissions doctrine claims that letting people die is not subject to the same absolute moral prohibition as deliberately killing them. Thus, for instance, active euthanasia (administering drugs to kill a patient) is forbidden, while passive euthanasia (withholding treatment that would keep her alive) is not. How does this moral distinction stand up to scrutiny?

POSITIVE AND NEGATIVE DUTIES
In contrasting doing X and allowing X to happen, the act that would have

TIMELINE

1930

Sir David Ross gives an account of morality in terms of *prima facie* duties

1967

Philippa Foot analyses acts and omissions in terms of positive and negative duties prevented X occurring must be something that I could have done and might reasonably be expected to do. The degree of moral censure involved, if any, then depends on the kind of obligation, or duty, to which this expectation gives rise. Taking this lead, the English philosopher Philippa Foot analyses the acts and omissions distinction in terms of rights and duties that mirror the *prima facie* duties set forth by Sir David Ross (*see page 56*).

Like Ross, Foot believes that there are competing duties that must be weighed against each other in reaching moral judgments. Everybody, she suggests, has a (weak) positive right to be benefited and a (strong) negative right not to be harmed. Corresponding to these rights there are duties: a (weak) positive duty to benefit others and a (strong) negative duty not to harm others. Doing harm, in these terms, consists in violating someone's negative right not to be harmed, while allowing harm consists in violating someone's positive right to be benefited (or saved from harm).

Foot imagines two medical situations where conflict of negative and positive duties seems to explain our differing intuitions. Suppose that there is a scarce drug that a doctor can use to save the life either of one man who requires a large dose or five men who require smaller doses. In this case it is a matter of weighing the positive duty to bring aid to one against the similar duty to bring aid to five, and, other things being equal, it is right (so most people

Playing God

In matters of life and death, the acts and omissions doctrine may play on our fear that by actively doing something we are 'playing God': deciding who should live and who should die. If we allow a woman and her unborn child to die, rather than saving her by carrying out an abortion, we can at least comfort ourselves that we are letting nature run its course – that we are leaving the matter in God's hands. But this should be small consolation. For in what morally relevant sense is 'sitting back and doing nothing' actually doing nothing? A decision not to act is as much a decision as it is to act, so it appears that in such cases we have no choice but to play God – and to accept the moral consequences of the choices we make.

1975

James Rachels argues that there is no moral distinction between doing and allowing to happen

2009

United Nations reports that 17,000 children die of hunger every day judge) to do as much good as possible by saving as many lives as possible. However, it would be wrong if the only means of bringing about the same outcome was to kill a man and harvest his organs for transplant into the five patients. In this case the positive duty to aid the five is outweighed by the negative duty not to bring harm to the one.

KILLING COUSINS

Are there situations in which allowing something to happen is as morally culpable as doing something? The American philosopher James Rachels believes that there are and supports his contention by inviting us to consider the following two cases:

(A) *Smith stands to gain a large inheritance by the death of his young cousin. One evening, while the child is taking a bath, he sneaks into the bathroom and drowns him.*

(B) *Jones also stands to gain by his cousin's death. He sneaks into the bathroom, intending to drown the child, but just as he does so, the child slips, hits his head and falls face-down in the bathwater. Jones stand over the bath, ready to push the child under if necessary, but it is not necessary: the child drowns as Jones looks on and does nothing.*

Smith actively does harm to the child, so violating his negative right not to be harmed, while Jones 'merely' allows harm to happen, violating the child's positive right to be benefited. According to Foot's analysis, we ought to find Smith's behaviour morally worse than Jones's, but – in Rachels's view – we do not: we regard what they do as equally wrong.

A GUIDE THAT IS NO GUIDE

Rachels believes that these cases show that there is no morally significant difference between doing harm and allowing harm to happen. It is doubtful that he has proved this much – his examples indicate only that allowing *can*

Shaky defence

We take a dim view of parents who murder their children, whether they do it by poisoning them or starving them to death. There is a very great distance, it is generally supposed, between such heinous acts and allowing millions of impoverished children around the world to die of starvation each year. This commonplace omission, easily tolerated by many of us most of the time, is a great deal less contemptible, morally speaking, than achieving the same result by sending poisoned food. Or is it? The effort needed to prevent such an outcome may be rather more strenuous, but the outcome itself is hardly less certain. Is the moral distance really so great? We like to think so, but if the mitigating factors are degree of exertion and wilful ignorance, the defence is little better in ethics than it is in law.

be as bad as doing. Still, if we agree that cases such as those given by Rachels are *exceptions* to the acts and omissions doctrine, this very fact does grievous damage to it. If a principle allows exceptions, it means that every case to which the principle is applied must be examined to see if it is one of the exceptions. Such a principle is, arguably, not a principle at all, and whatever it is, it is certainly not much help in offering moral guidance.

The condensed idea
Doing and allowing to happen

17 Moral luck

Sisters Phoebe and Millie are both quite set on getting rid of their feckless husbands. Phoebe sneaks back home late at night, grabs a knife from the kitchen table, tiptoes up to the bedroom, and gleefully plunges the blade into her snoring husband's chest. At the same moment, Millie sneaks back home, grabs a knife from the kitchen table, tiptoes upstairs, and gleefully thrusts it at her snoring husband, only to see the blade of her son's toy knife collapse as it strikes his chest.

The law takes a very different view of each sister's behaviour. Phoebe has committed murder and, if caught and convicted, is likely to spend many or most of her remaining years behind bars. Millie, on the other hand, will face a charge of attempted murder, at worst, even supposing that her bungled effort is treated with that degree of seriousness. In any case, it is a less grave offence, and any punishment she receives will be proportionately less severe.

The law, then, clearly regards the outcome of an action to be relevant in assessing its gravity as an offence. The successful murderer is held to have done something considerably worse than her less competent sister. A similar distinction is recognized in other areas of the law. Consider, for instance, the case of two drivers, each driving recklessly, one of whom happens to hit and kill a child. Again, the action of the child-killer is held to be much more culpable, and he is likely to be much more severely punished as a consequence.

TIMELINE

5th century BC	1947
The legend of Oedipus, king of Thebes, is told by the Greek tragedian Sophocles and others	Rudolf Höss, commandant at Auschwitz till 1943, is found guilty of war crimes and hanged

We expect, or at least hope, that the law is a fairly faithful mirror of morality. So to what extent does the legal view accord with our common moral intuitions? The child-killing driver is likely to judge *himself* much more harshly than his more fortunate double, and most of us would doubtless agree with him. In the same way, the successfully murderous sister would generally be considered to have done something significantly worse than her less competent sister.

An example used by the American philosopher Thomas Nagel neatly captures our ambivalence in such matters:

> If one negligently leaves the bath running with the baby in it, one
> will realize, as one bounds up the stairs towards the bathroom, that
> if the baby has drowned one has done something awful, whereas if it
> has not one has merely been careless.

IS IT BAD TO BE UNLUCKY?

In fact, our normal intuitions, and the law too, seem to be rather confused in these cases. For we usually suppose that two people should not be judged differently unless the differences are due to factors that they can control: blame and praise should be reserved for things that are done voluntarily. I will take a dim view of your deliberately throwing coffee over me, but I will be less quick to blame you if you slipped or someone jogged your elbow. However, in the cases considered above, it is a matter of pure chance that one driver kills and the other does not, that one sister succeeds and the other does not. The only thing that seems to make a difference is luck, and luck is, by definition, outside our control.

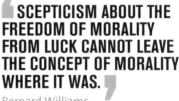

SCEPTICISM ABOUT THE FREEDOM OF MORALITY FROM LUCK CANNOT LEAVE THE CONCEPT OF MORALITY WHERE IT WAS.

Bernard Williams,
Moral Luck, 1981

1979

Thomas Nagel suggests
that everyday morality is
not immune to luck

1981

Bernard Williams's *Moral Luck*
questions the tie between morality
and voluntariness

No room for regret

Imagine that you were involved in an appalling accident. Suppose, for instance, you were driving with all 'due care and attention' – at a safe speed, in a car that you had taken every reasonable precaution to make roadworthy, and so on – and yet were unlucky enough to run over a child who ran out into the road in front of you. Assuming that the accident was purely down to bad luck – that there really was nothing you could have done to prevent it – the normal view, both in law and in common morality, would be that you were free of blame: your action was involuntary and therefore outside the scope of legal or moral censure. For most of us, however, this would be small consolation indeed: we would surely be consumed by remorse, deeply regretting both the death of the child and the fact that we had played a part in bringing it about. Is such regret unreasonable or irrational or misplaced? Try telling that to the unlucky driver. Much modern ethical theory, focusing mainly on actions rather than agents, fails to give an adequate account of the phenomenon of agent regret. The ancient Greeks, whose ethical understanding began in the character of the agent, knew better: they realized that there was nothing unreasonable, and everything human, in Oedipus' overwhelming anguish when he discovers that, entirely against his will, he has married his mother and killed his father.

It looks, then, as if the link between blame and voluntariness – or control – is less firm than we generally suppose. We seem to blame people not only for what they do voluntarily but also for what they do as a matter of luck. It appears that morality is not immune to chance after all and that there is such a thing as moral luck: bad luck, apparently, can make you bad.

OR IS IT UNLUCKY TO BE BAD?

We might seem to be on safer ground to judge people on the basis of their intentions, rather than the outcome of those intentions. Such a move would obviously change our evaluations of the murderous sisters and the reckless drivers. But even then the problem of luck does not disappear, for we may wonder to what extent we really have control over our intentions.

We form the intentions we form because of the kinds of people we are, and there are innumerable factors that shape us as people that we cannot control. Our character is the product of an enormously complex combination of genetic and environmental factors over which we have little or no control. So to what extent should we be judged for actions or intentions that flow naturally from our character? If I can't help being cowardly or selfish – if it is, as it were, 'in my nature' to be so – is it fair to blame or criticize me for running away from danger or thinking too much of my own interests?

It is possible to keep pushing back the boundaries of luck further and further. Often an evaluation of moral badness appears to depend purely on being in the wrong place at the wrong time. We can display the good and bad points of our characters only if circumstances provide us with opportunities to do so. You cannot show your great natural generosity if you lack the resources to be generous with or the potential beneficiaries to be generous to. We may think that we would never have displayed the depravity of a Nazi guard at Auschwitz, but of course we will never know that for sure. All we can say for certain is that we are very fortunate that we will never have to find out. So was the Nazi guard unfortunate that he was put in a situation where he could find out? Was he unlucky to be bad?

Taken to its logical conclusion, the debate over whether there is such a thing as moral luck merges with the issue of free will and raises the same questions: in the final analysis, is *anything* we do done freely, and if there is no freedom, can there be responsibility? And without responsibility, what justification is there for blame and punishment?

The condensed idea
Untying the moral
and the voluntary

18 Free will

The concept of free will – the idea that we are free agents, able to act as we please – is fundamental to all ethical thinking. If I say that you *should* do such and such, I imply that you *can* do it. It is because you are able (or thought to be able) to do other than you do that it makes sense to hold you accountable for your actions: you can be praised, and perhaps rewarded, for doing one thing; and blamed, and perhaps punished, for doing another. But if free will is an illusion – if we are never really free to do other than we do – the idea of moral choice and responsibility seems to be drained of meaning.

There is no doubt that we all habitually think and behave as if we have freedom in this sense. The problem is that there are powerful reasons for supposing that the universe is essentially deterministic, meaning that everything that happens is fixed by a necessary chain of causation. If this is so, all human actions, as events in the universe, are determined too and could not be other than they are.

So, if we live in such a universe, does it mean that we lack free will and hence are not distinctively moral beings, fully responsible for our actions? Is there any point in deliberating over anything we do, if the result of our deliberation is fixed in advance? What place, indeed, is there for gratitude and resentment in such a world? Why be thankful for, or resentful of, something that could not have been otherwise?

TIMELINE

4th–3rd century BC	3rd century BC
Greek Epicurus introduces uncaused 'swerve' to allow free will in his atomistic world-view	Greek Stoic philosophers embrace a strong form of cosmic determinism

COGS IN A CLOCKWORK UNIVERSE

Although its origins can be traced back to the ancient Greeks, the modern understanding of determinism owes much to the mechanistic view of the universe that began with the work of Isaac Newton in the 17th century. In the Newtonian, or 'clockwork', universe, everything behaves necessarily according to fixed physical laws. Just as the movements of a clock's hands can be predicted once it has been wound and set in motion, so every succeeding state of the universe follows inevitably once the initial conditions have been established. Thus the future history of the universe was fixed for all time at the moment of its inception.

Assuming that we (as physical denizens of the universe) are subject to deterministic laws, it follows that everything we do – every decision we make, every thought we entertain, our every intention, desire and motivation – is fixed by some preceding state. This causal chain can be followed back, in principle, to some state for which we clearly have no responsibility (things that happened before we were born, for example). Any future state that we bring about is *already* determined by an earlier state and the laws of nature. If that is so, how can we possibly be held responsible for that state?

PHILOSOPHERS ON FREE WILL

The threat to free will posed by determinism has elicited a wide range of philosophical responses. Among these a number of distinct approaches can be seen.

If your number's up ...

Determinism is sometimes, rather despairingly, confused with fatalism, the view that 'what will be will be' and that human action is ineffectual. If everything is fixed in advance, why bother to do anything about it? You are going to die sooner or later, so why bother to give up smoking? In fact, whether you die sooner or later may well depend on whether you stop smoking. Whether you give up or not may be fixed in advance, as may your term of life, and the two facts may be connected: none of which goes to show that human action has no influence over events.

1687

Newton's *Principia Mathematica* lays the foundations for the mechanistic understanding of the universe

1814

Pierre-Simon Laplace gives the first published account of scientific or causal determinism

Explaining evil in the world

For many people, especially in time of personal trauma, the 'problem of evil' – the presence of pain and suffering in the world – is the most serious challenge to the idea of an all-loving God. Historically, the most important theological response to this challenge is the so-called 'free will defence'. The divine gift of free will, it is argued, allows us to make genuine choices for ourselves, and this means that we can live lives of real moral worth and so enter into a deep relationship of love and trust with God. However, God could not have made this gift to us without the risk of our abusing it – of our misusing our freedom to make the wrong choices. It was a risk worth taking and a price worth paying, but God could not have eliminated the possibility of moral baseness without depriving us of a greater gift – the capacity for moral goodness. Of course, if we are not in fact free to make real choices in our lives, as determinism suggests, the free will defence quickly unravels.

Hard determinists accept that determinism is true and that it is incompatible with free will: our actions are causally determined and the idea that we are free, in the sense that we could have acted differently, is illusory. Thus they believe that moral censure and praise, as normally conceived, are inappropriate.

In contrast, soft determinists (or compatibilists), while accepting that determinism is true, deny that it is incompatible with free will. The fact that we could have acted differently *if we had chosen* gives a satisfactory and sufficient notion of freedom of action. It is irrelevant, in their view, that a choice is causally determined; the important point is that it is not coerced or contrary to our wishes. An action that is free in this sense is open to normal moral assessment.

Libertarians agree with hard determinists that determinism is incompatible with free will, but rather than deny the possibility of free will, they reject determinism. They maintain that soft determinism's claim that we could have acted differently if we had chosen is empty, because not making such a choice is itself causally determined (or would be if determinism were true). The libertarian thus holds that our choices and actions are not determined and hence that human free will is real.

The problem for libertarians is to explain how an action can occur indeterminately – in particular, how an uncaused event can avoid being random. It has been suggested that the notion of free will might be saved by quantum theory, according to which events at the subatomic level are uncaused or indeterminate – they are matters of pure chance that 'just happen'. But the essence of quantum indeterminacy is randomness, so the idea that our actions and choices are at some profound level random appears to be no less damaging to the idea of moral responsibility than determinism.

> [DETERMINISM] PROFESSES THAT THOSE PARTS OF THE UNIVERSE ALREADY LAID DOWN ABSOLUTELY APPOINT AND DECREE WHAT THE OTHER PARTS SHALL BE.
>
> William James, 'The Dilemma of Determinism', 1884

THE METAPHYSICAL ELEPHANT IN THE ROOM

The spectre of determinism looms over ethics, unexorcized after centuries of debate. The basic issue – the fact that our perception of ourselves as moral beings is apparently at odds with the scientific understanding of the universe – continues to divide philosophers, and no consensus is in sight. Metaphysical questions – questions about the fundamental nature of things – are sometimes dismissed as pie in the sky (sometimes almost literally), but the implications of determinism have proved harder to sweep aside.

The condensed idea
Are we really free?

The social contract

Why should we obey the state and the laws that it lays down? The answer is that we agree to do so. Collectively, hypothetically, perhaps even historically – the precise nature of the agreement is obscure – we have given our consent to the state's authority in return for the benefits it brings us. These may include security from threats, freedom to do as we please without interference, and justice, in the broad sense of a fair and proper distribution of wealth and other goods within society.

Such, at least, is the basic understanding of social contract theory. The idea that the state's institutions and structures are established on the basis of an agreement or 'social contract' between its members was first suggested by the English political theorist Thomas Hobbes in his treatise *Leviathan* (1651). The theory has two central features: consent and rationality. It is the consent of the governed that gives the state legitimacy – recognition of its power and authority to make laws. And it is rational consideration of their own interests that leads the citizens of the state to assent to its authority: cooperation, achieved by agreeing to abide by laws that apply equally to all, is the surest means for each member to look after his or her own interests.

If you willingly sign a contract, it must be that you think you will be better off, on balance, being bound by its terms than you would be otherwise. You probably don't like paying a large sum of money to your bank every month, but you prefer it to the alternative – not having a house – so you sign a mortgage contract. Your preference in this case is, or should be, a rational

TIMELINE

1651	1690
Thomas Hobbes makes the first and most influential statement of the social contract theory	John Locke's *Two Treatises of Government* argues the case for constitutional monarchy

one: consideration of your position and interests, with and without the contract, leads you to make a commitment that you would not otherwise choose to make.

HOBBES AND LEVIATHAN

In a similar vein, Hobbes begins his analysis of the social contract by considering how things would stand without the state to which it gives rise. He evokes a hypothetical pre-social condition of mankind which he calls the 'state of nature', a vision that is unremittingly bleak. He assumes that people are driven exclusively by self-interest – acting in isolation, they are concerned only with their own pleasure and preservation; their prime motivation 'a perpetual and restless desire of power after power, that ceaseth only in death'. With people constantly in conflict and competition with one another, there is no possibility of trust or cooperation; and with no basis of trust, there is no prospect of creating prosperity or enjoying the fruits of civilization: 'No arts; no letters; no society; and which is worst of all, continual fear, and danger of violent death.' And hence, Hobbes famously concludes, in the state of nature 'the life of man [is] solitary, poor, nasty, brutish, and short'.

Everyone has an interest in working together to escape the hellish scene painted by Hobbes, so why might people in the state of nature not agree to cooperate? The answer is that there is never enough trust to get started. There is always a cost to pay in complying with an agreement and always something to be gained from not doing so. If self-interest is the only thing that motivates people, as Hobbes suggests, there will always be someone ready to seek an advantage by reneging on the deal. In the circumstances, the best you can do is to break the contract first – and everyone else reasons in the same way, of course, so there is no trust and any prospective agreement quickly unravels. Long-term interest is always sure to give way to short-term gain, apparently leaving no way out of the cycle of distrust and violence.

1762

Jean-Jacques Rousseau, in *The Social Contract*, proposes that the state owes its authority to the general will of the governed

1971

John Rawls develops idea of justice as fairness in *A Theory of Justice*

Behind the veil of ignorance

The most prominent social contract theorist of the 20th century was the US political philosopher John Rawls. In *A Theory of Justice* (1971), Rawls introduces a thought experiment that is clearly in the tradition of Hobbes's state of nature. Rawls imagines a hypothetical situation (the 'original position') in which individuals are placed behind a 'veil of ignorance', which obscures all personal interests and allegiances: 'No one knows his place in society, his class position or social status, nor does anyone know his fortune in the distribution of natural assets and abilities, his intelligence, strength, and the like.' Placed behind the veil and ignorant of what society has in store for us, we are obliged to play safe and ensure that no one group is given an advantage at the expense of another. As in Hobbes, it is purely rational self-interest that drives decision-making behind the veil. It is the fact that we, when placed in this position, contract into certain social and economic structures and arrangements that makes them just and hence socially stable and robust.

How, then, can individuals locked in such miserable discord ever reach an agreement and so extricate themselves? The crux of the problem, for Hobbes, is that 'covenants, without the sword, are but words'. What is needed is an external power or sanction that *forces* everybody to abide by the terms of a contract that benefits them all. People must willingly restrict their liberties for the sake of cooperation and peace, on condition that everyone else does likewise; they must 'confer all their power and strength upon one man, or upon one assembly of men, that may reduce all their wills, by plurality of voices, unto one will'. The solution, then, is joint submission to the absolute authority of the state (what Hobbes calls 'Leviathan') – 'a common power to keep them all in awe'.

LOCKE ON GOVERNMENT BY CONSENT

Nearly half a century after Hobbes, another great English philosopher, John Locke, picked up the idea of the social contract to explore the basis of government. Locke's conception of the state of nature is considerably less bleak than Hobbes's, so the contract he envisages between people and sovereign is markedly less draconian. Whereas Hobbes requires the state's power to be unlimited and absolute in order to stave off the horrors of the 'war of all against all', Locke makes the case for what is essentially constitutional monarchy. In his view, the people consent to make over their power to the sovereign on condition that he uses it for the common good, and they reserve the right to withdraw that consent if the sovereign fails in his contractual duties. The forceful overthrow of the government by the people, by rebellion if necessary, remains a legitimate (albeit final) remedy.

CONTRACT CRITICISMS

Social contract theory is open to criticism on several fronts. If the making of the original contract is supposed (rather implausibly) to be a real historical event, we may wonder why we should be bound by consent given by our ancestors. One response is to suggest that we give our (tacit) consent merely by our participation in society, by enjoying the benefits it offers. But what other options are open to us? A legal contract requires that the parties to it participate voluntarily, but in the case of the social contract, not only are other alternatives unavailable, but the state typically uses its powers to force compliance.

There is also the difficulty that the social contract apparently excludes many we might wish to include. Even allowing that consent has been, or could be, given, what of those who are not competent to give such consent? We would have to exclude people with severe intellectual impairments, and no consideration need be given to future generations of human beings. And what of the poor and the dispossessed? If the state is some kind of bargain struck between its members, why should those in society who enjoy few of its benefits be obliged to obey its rules?

Perhaps the most vulnerable aspect of Hobbes's version of the theory is his contention that human beings are purely egoistical – that they always act solely in their own self-interest. Against this view, evolutionary and other scientific evidence suggests that people are fundamentally social animals, with natural impulses towards altruism and cooperation. If this is so, the need for a social contract that explains how and why we live together begins to evaporate.

The condensed idea
Society by contract

20 Virtue ethics

Since the Enlightenment – for some three-and-a-half centuries – most moral philosophers have supposed that their main task is to explain ethical behaviour, not to analyse virtuous character. They have tended to focus primarily on actions, not agents – on what sort of things we should *do* rather than what sort of people we should *be*. To this end they have attempted to discover the principles on which moral obligation depends and to formulate rules that guide us to behave in accordance with these principles.

That is not to say that the idea of virtue has been excluded from ensuing discussions of moral philosophy, but it has sometimes been seen as secondary or instrumental: as a disposition that helps us to do what duty requires, for instance, or as a means of achieving some ulterior goal such as utility or well-being. But it wasn't always the case – virtue has not always played handmaiden to duty or some other good beyond itself.

For the great thinkers of classical Greece, primarily Plato and Aristotle, the main concern within ethics was the nature of virtue (moral excellence) and the cultivation of good character. The principal question, in their view, was not 'What is the right thing to do?' but 'What is the best way to live?' The Greeks' concern with excellence of character was dominant until the start of the early modern period, when it was largely set aside (along with Aristotle's philosophy) for several centuries. From the middle of the 20th century, however, some thinkers began to express their dissatisfaction with

early 4th century BC

Plato asserts that virtue is
identical with knowledge

mid-4th century BC

Aristotle's ethics prioritizes the
cultivation of good character

the prevailing trend in moral philosophy and to revive interest in the study of character and virtues. This recent movement, together with the older views from which it takes its inspiration, is known as 'virtue ethics'.

THE GREEKS ON VIRTUE

According to Aristotle, being a good person is not primarily a matter of doing the right kind of things or understanding certain rules and principles. Rather, it is a question of being or becoming the kind of person who, by acquiring wisdom through proper practice and training, habitually behaves in appropriate ways in the appropriate circumstances. In short, having the right kind of character and dispositions, natural and acquired, results in the right kind of behaviour. The dispositions in question are virtues. These are expressions or manifestations of *eudaimonia*, which the Greeks took to be the highest good for man and the ultimate purpose of human activity. Usually translated as 'happiness', *eudaimonia* is broader than this and less subjective, best captured by the idea of 'flourishing' or 'enjoying a good (successful, fortunate) life'.

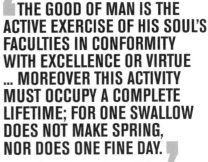

THE GOOD OF MAN IS THE ACTIVE EXERCISE OF HIS SOUL'S FACULTIES IN CONFORMITY WITH EXCELLENCE OR VIRTUE … MOREOVER THIS ACTIVITY MUST OCCUPY A COMPLETE LIFETIME; FOR ONE SWALLOW DOES NOT MAKE SPRING, NOR DOES ONE FINE DAY.

Aristotle, *Nichomachean Ethics*, fourth century BC

The Greeks often talk about four cardinal virtues – courage, justice, temperance (self-mastery) and intelligence (practical wisdom) – but a pivotal doctrine for both Plato and Aristotle is the so-called 'unity of the virtues'. Starting from the observation that a good person must recognize how to respond sensitively to the sometimes conflicting demands of different virtues, they conclude that the virtues are like different facets of a single jewel, so it is not in fact possible to hold one virtue without having them all. In Aristotle, the possession and cultivation of all the various virtues means that the good man is 'great-souled' (*megalopsychos*), a model of goodness and virtue.

17th century	1958
The start of the Enlightenment sees the eclipse of the Aristotelian approach to ethics	Anscombe's essay 'Modern Moral Philosophy' sparks the modern revival of virtue ethics

Aristotle and the golden mean

'Virtue,' wrote Aristotle in his *Nichomachean Ethics*, 'is a state of character concerned with choice, lying in the mean which is defined by reference to reason. It is a mean between two vices, one of excess and one of deficiency.' Aristotle's conception of virtue as a mean is sometimes mistakenly linked with the famous inscription at the temple of Apollo at Delphi: *mēden agan*, 'Nothing in excess.' But the idea that we should be 'moderate in all things' is not what Aristotle has in mind. Far from suggesting that we should always, unthinkingly, strike a middle path, he insists that the mean is to be defined strictly by reason, which should govern our baser, non-rational instincts. For example: the virtue that lies as a mean between cowardice and rashness is courage. Being courageous is not only a matter of avoiding cowardly actions such as running away from the enemy, it is also necessary to avoid foolhardy, devil-may-care bravado, such as mounting a futile attack that will be damaging to oneself and one's comrades. The key point is that whatever we do should be *appropriate* to the circumstances, as determined by practical wisdom responding sensitively to the particular facts of the situation.

Plato finally moves beyond unity to identity, concluding that the different virtues are in fact one and the same and that they are subsumed under a single virtue – knowledge. The idea that virtue is (identical with) knowledge led Plato to deny the possibility of *akrasia*, or weakness of will: for him, it was impossible to 'know the better yet do the worse'; to behave intemperately, for instance, was not a matter of weakness but of ignorance. (Aristotle, always wary of straying too far from common beliefs, rejected this view.) For Plato and Aristotle, behaving virtuously was inextricably linked to the exercise of reason, or rational choice; and Aristotle elaborated this idea into the influential doctrine of the (golden) mean (*see box*).

MODERN VIRTUE ETHICS

A major catalyst for the modern revival of virtue ethics was the article 'Modern Moral Philosophy', written in 1958 by the English philosopher Elizabeth Anscombe. In this essay she captures a growing dissatisfaction with the prevailing forms of ethical theory, principally utilitarianism and Kantianism. Her main objection to these theories is that they maintain the 'law conception of ethics' – they focus on concepts such as 'morally ought' and 'morally obligated' – and yet dispense with the divine source of authority (God) that gives sense to these concepts.

It is arguable that Anscombe – herself a staunch Roman Catholic – was objecting to the secularity of prevailing theories and was recommending instead a return to some kind of religiously based moral theory. Be that as it may, many philosophers inspired by her work have assumed that her target is the 'law conception' itself – that is, the legislative structure of moral obligation – and hence that she was advocating the kind of secular ethics characteristic of the ancient Greeks. Deliberately or not, Anscombe lent impetus to a new generation of virtue ethicists, who, taking their lead from Aristotle and others, have developed theories in which such ideas as moral character, practical wisdom and virtue itself are prioritized.

The condensed idea
Who you are, not what you do

21 Humanism

What is the meaning of life? For those with religious faith, the answer is, in a sense, simple: the purpose of our life on Earth is to serve God (or gods). It may not always be simple to divine the will of God or to interpret the scriptures through which God's intentions are conveyed to us. Still, the aim – to satisfy God's wishes – is clear. But what if we do not have such faith? Then there is no easy answer, no straightforward path. Humanists are people who seek to live meaningful lives without religion; they do this in many ways, so – while they may share a broadly similar outlook on the world – their beliefs and values do not form a single doctrine or ideology.

The truths of religion, it is usually claimed, are based on the directly revealed word of God, so with God comes a great deal of certainty about many of life's most profound questions: the origin and nature of the world, the place of human beings in it and their relationship to other creatures, the way people should live and behave. The main motivation behind humanism is the belief that there is no God, so for humanists all these are open questions. Dispensing with the certainties of religion, they attempt to find answers for themselves.

THE DIGNITY OF MAN

From a religious perspective, a good life is one that is lived as God wishes us to live it; to do the right thing is to do as God has ordained. Ultimately, then, the source of value in our lives lies outside or beyond this world. Believing that there is no God, humanists cannot look to any such external source. For them, this world is all there is, this life is all we have: if we are to do any good in it or make anything valuable of it, we must do it here and now.

The value of life, then – why it matters and why it is worth living – must be located within this world, and in particular within human nature itself. Morality – which the religious might regard as arbitrary or relativistic without the authority of God – is, in the humanist view, rooted in human nature. A moral sense is an intrinsic part of that nature, founded on a concern for others and trust in their essential worth and on the value of society and friendship. The humanist's 'faith', then, is in humanity itself – in what the Renaissance humanists called the 'dignity of man'. It is not a blind faith,

Humanist enlightenments

Although the Greeks had their gods, their usual view, typified by Aristotle in particular, was that human flourishing depended on people realizing their potential on Earth by leading a life of virtue informed by reason. The Stoic philosophers, too, were often close in spirit to modern humanism: they believed that we could achieve inner contentment by living in harmony with nature and in conformity with reason, which was in their view the organizing principle of the universe. The project of understanding the human condition without reference to the divine gained momentum from the 15th century, when Renaissance thinkers such as Erasmus began to celebrate the essential dignity of mankind – though they attempted to do so without rejecting God as their creator. Tension between religious and humanist views intensified further from the 17th century, as the scientific revolution gathered pace and Enlightenment thinkers challenged the authority of the Church to control the lives of its followers, proclaiming that people had the right to think and choose for themselves.

17th century	**1859**	**2002**
Enlightenment thinkers challenge the Church's authority	Darwin's theory of evolution overturns the notion of mankind's divine origins	The revised Amsterdam Declaration sets out the principles of world humanism

A different spiritualism

Religious people give priority to their spiritual side, so it is perhaps not surprising that they tend to portray those who do not believe in God as lacking this dimension. It is doubtless true that some people respond to what they believe to be a godless universe by devoting themselves to material concerns, but it need not be so. The Amsterdam Declaration of 2002 – the nearest thing that humanism has to a statement of its principles – highlights the significance that humanists attach to 'artistic creativity and imagination'. It recognizes 'the transforming power of art' and affirms 'the importance of literature, music, and the visual and performing arts for personal development and fulfilment'. In fact, humanism is a way of looking at the world that extends back almost as far as humanity itself and has been the inspiration not only for philosophers and scientists but for numerous artists and writers.

however. Humanists are not unaware that people are frail and fallible, but they tend to be optimistic in their view that the better side of their nature will generally prevail.

FAITH IN LIBERTY, AUTONOMY AND SCIENCE

The project of living a purposeful life without religion does not entail any particular ideological position. The significance attached to human dignity, however, puts humanism firmly in a liberal tradition, and in practice humanists tend to share liberal values. Their central concern is that people are able to make the most of themselves, leading happy and fulfilled lives, and to this end they need the opportunity to develop fully as individuals. Essential to this are the prime liberal values of liberty and autonomy: as much freedom to think and express themselves as is compatible with the same freedom for others; and the right to make decisions on their own account and to control the course of their own lives.

Religions are dogmatic in their claims – the word of God is not negotiable or open to debate and the truths revealed in holy scriptures are meant to be absolute and fixed for all time. Especially in their fundamentalist forms, religions do not hesitate to restrict freedoms thought to offend against the will of God. The humanistic world-view, by contrast, rejecting dogmatic certainties, is provisional and speculative. Politically, humanists are likely to be opposed to authoritarian and paternalistic positions; in general they are committed to the liberal virtues of free speech and expression, equal rights, pluralism, toleration and democracy.

As atheists, humanists do not accept the supernatural accounts of the universe and the place of human beings within it that are given by religions. For them, the world is a natural phenomenon, not a divine creation, and as such it is open to rational explanation and inquiry. In particular, they are committed to a post-Darwinian view of *Homo sapiens* as one of many animal species – a notably intelligent species, to be sure, but not different in essence or kind from any other. In general, humanists look to science as the most reliable means of attaining knowledge; they trust in science's characteristic method, which involves positing hypotheses that explain the available evidence and which are then subjected to a continuing process of confirmation, revision and rejection. Where the religious mindset is dogmatic and certain, the humanist outlook is always sceptical and open to amendment.

> **A MAN'S ETHICAL BEHAVIOUR SHOULD BE BASED EFFECTUALLY ON SYMPATHY, EDUCATION AND SOCIAL TIES; NO RELIGIOUS BASIS IS NECESSARY.**
>
> Albert Einstein, *The New York Times Magazine*, 1930

The condensed idea
Finding purpose without God

22 Nihilism

Derived from the Latin word for 'nothing' (*nihil*), nihilism means 'belief in nothing'. In matters of ethics, the most extreme sense is that nothing has any value – that nothing is right or wrong, that life has no meaning or purpose. This profoundly bleak outlook gives the word negative connotations, and it is often used in a hostile manner against those who reject or do not share a particular set of values.

The word 'nihilism' has also been attached to a number of other, less extreme positions. Believing in nothing may amount to *not* believing in anything, but it is not a big stretch to see this as believing in *anything*. Accordingly, positions as diverse as moral scepticism (which questions whether ethical truths can be known) and moral relativism (which proposes that all values are relative to a particular culture, time, etc.) are sometimes described as nihilistic.

NIHILISM AS ANTI-REALISM

Most commonly, as a philosophical position, ethical nihilism amounts to a rejection of moral realism: the idea, in its simplest form, that moral values are objective facts that exist independently of us and that the truth of ethical claims (like scientific ones) depends on their correspondence with this external reality (*see chapter 4*). Nihilism, then, denies this picture and proposes that there are no such things as right and wrong, in the sense that there are no moral values that justify claims made in these terms. Such claims and judgments are simply mistaken, and morality as usually understood is an illusion.

TIMELINE

1880s–90s	1927
Nihilistic ideas are explored in Friedrich Nietzsche's published and unpublished works	Martin Heidegger's *Being and Time* becomes a seminal existentialist text

Nihilism, in this qualified sense, is basically equivalent to anti-realism, and may be no more than a staging post to some subjectivist account of ethics (*see chapter 5*). However, there are also richer, more substantive ideas that are called nihilistic – beliefs about the essential nature and limitations of the human condition. These ideas are associated in particular with the 19th-century German philosopher Friedrich Nietzsche and, in the following century, with the existentialists.

'GOD IS DEAD'

Nietzsche is a nihilist in the sense outlined above, in that he believes that the world has no objective structure. There is simply no 'true world', he says – no external reality to which our beliefs more or less faithfully correspond. There is no truth, in this sense; reason is impotent; and our supposed knowledge of the world is only ever perspectival – that is, essentially grounded in some or other perspective on it. According to this view, all there is to the world is what we choose to give it – no values are absolute, all are without foundation and humanly constructed or created.

THE MARK OF NIHILISM IS INDIFFERENCE TO LIFE.

Albert Camus, *The Rebel*, 1951

There is more to Nietzsche's nihilism than this, however. Living a life, for Nietzsche, requires an active commitment to fashioning values – values that give life its meaning and reinforce the 'will to power': the instinct that drives a person to thrive and grow. Such values, created over time and shared within a culture, are preserved and enforced by its social institutions, until such time as they no longer serve their purpose and cease to be 'life-affirming'. A nihilistic phase then ensues in which these values, now life-denying, are exposed as mere superstition. The cycle is then completed as new values are constructed in their place.

1942

Albert Camus's essay *The Myth of Sisyphus* explores the doctrine of the absurd

1943

Jean-Paul Sartre's most significant philosophical work, *Being and Nothingness*, is published

Nihilists under attack

People who have firm opinions on moral matters, whether based on religious or philosophical conviction, tend to present those who reject their views as believing in nothing and hence refer to them as nihilists. And because people with a fixed outlook on life typically have a clear view of what gives their own life meaning, they may suppose that their opponents lack such a view – that their lives are pointless and morally bankrupt. However, although nihilists may seek to undermine conventional or traditional views and deny the existence of absolute moral standards, the more interesting of them develop ideas or strategies to explain how we might extricate ourselves from (or at least survive amid) the rubble of our former opinions.

Nietzsche believed that the world of his own day, in the final decades of the 19th century, was undergoing its greatest crisis of nihilism. The quest for truth characteristic of the Enlightenment and the scientific revolution had exposed, by working through the implications of its own inner logic, the lack of foundations for that truth; the very values that underpinned modernity's striving for progress were threatening to undermine their own foundations ('the highest values devalue themselves,' as Nietzsche puts it). He called this great crisis of humanity – the disintegration of its social, political and moral basis; the loss of purpose and meaning; the triumph of nihilism – the 'death of God'. He was not without hope that the crisis could be overcome, that life could be reaffirmed. But not yet: for people, unconscious of the catastrophe unfolding around them, continued to cling to outworn convictions, including the life-denying pieties of religion.

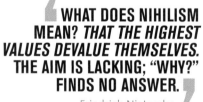

WHAT DOES NIHILISM MEAN? *THAT THE HIGHEST VALUES DEVALUE THEMSELVES. THE AIM IS LACKING; "WHY?" FINDS NO ANSWER.*

Friedrich Nietzsche,
Will to Power, 1887

CONFRONTING FUTILITY

Nietzsche's nihilist views were enormously influential in the 20th century, not least on the existentialists – Jean-Paul Sartre, Albert Camus, Martin Heidegger among others – whose ideas shot to prominence in the decades following the Second World War. Atheistic like Nietzsche, they start from the view that there is no external source, God or other, to give life meaning or purpose. We are faced, instead, with absurdity: the brute fact of existence; the gratuitousness of life; the fact that we are thrown, willy-nilly, into an alien and uncaring universe.

It is this very indifference, according to Sartre, that makes us free to forge meaning for ourselves. Only by making significant choices about our lives – by creating values and asserting them in the face of indifference – can we live with 'authenticity'. Otherwise, failing to take up the responsibility of our freedom and to commit ourselves to creating meaning, we are condemned to live in 'bad faith'. But with absolute freedom comes anguish, consciousness of the effort to cope in the face of pointlessness. This is the pain and futility of existence that Camus dramatizes in *The Myth of Sisyphus* (1942): the figure of Greek myth, punished by the gods and condemned for eternity to push a boulder to the top of a hill, only to see it plunge back down just as it reaches the crest.

The condensed idea
Believing in nothing

23 Justice

'The sovereign mistress and queen of all the virtues,' wrote the Roman writer and politician Cicero on the subject of justice, 'the crowning glory' of moral excellence. Pre-eminent it may be, but justice is a complex idea. It is clearly a different thing for a person to be just and for a society to be just, and much philosophical debate has focused on how these different forms of justice are related.

At the core of most conceptions of justice is the idea of the distribution of good and bad things, broadly defined. The goods in question comprise all those things (benefits and resources, necessarily limited) that people consider valuable or worth having, such as property, wealth, reputation and position in society; the bad things include those burdens and obligations that people generally find undesirable and seek to avoid, such as poverty and taxation. The characteristic of a just person is to respect the goods of others, refraining from taking what belongs to them and insisting on returning what is owed to them. A just society, on the other hand, is one in which its members acknowledge that the distribution of goods within it is not arbitrary but just or fair. The critical question, then, is in what such fairness resides: should the distribution of goods among a society's members be equal, or should it, perhaps, be dependent on what they deserve?

THE GREEKS ON JUSTICE

The Greek philosopher Plato gives a highly distinctive account of justice, most fully presented in *The Republic*. He draws a parallel between social forms of justice and the individual – between justice in his ideal state and moral excellence (virtue) in individuals. Justice in the state, he proposes, resides in the three classes of citizens (rulers, guardians, producers) achieving a proper balance, or social harmony, in the performance of their duties; in the same way, the moral well-being of an individual depends on a proper balance, or inner harmony, between the three parts of the soul (reason, emotions, appetites). Thus, Plato's virtuous man, who (by analogy with the state) is also just, is guided by reason, and it is this that tempers worldly ambitions and bodily passions. Justice so conceived is an entirely internal disposition and is not related to any external factor, such as a person's readiness to comply with just social institutions and laws. It is also very much open-ended. Just actions are simply those prompted or sanctioned by a soul that is harmoniously balanced in the way that Plato describes.

> **JUSTICE IS THE CONSTANT AND PERPETUAL WILL TO RENDER TO OTHERS WHAT IS DUE TO THEM.**
> Emperor Justinian,
> sixth century AD

The most important influence on later accounts of justice was Plato's younger contemporary Aristotle, who identifies the essence of justice as people 'getting their due'. In contrast to the Platonic conception, Aristotle's justice is external, in that the idea of getting one's due requires some kind of external criterion, and it is distributive, in that it implies that everybody should get the share of good and bad things that they deserve or have a right to expect. The idea of balance or proportion is still present in Aristotle, but now the sense is limited to a balance between what people get and what they deserve. It is this idea of balance that is symbolized, in a legal context, by the pair of scales held by the figure of Justice personified.

WITHOUT FEAR OR FAVOUR

As well as carrying a pair of scales, Justice personified is blindfolded: she is required to be impartial and even-handed in her judgments. But justice cannot be blind to all differences: impartiality requires only that *irrelevant*

1971	**2009**
John Rawls sets out his theory of justice as fairness	Amartya Sen argues for a pluralistic understanding of justice

The fable of the flute

Three children are squabbling over who should get to keep a flute. Anne claims the instrument on the grounds that she is the only one of the three who knows how to play it. The second child, Bob, says that he should have it, because he is so poor that he has no other toys to play with. Finally, Carla claims that the flute should be hers, because it was she who made it. So who should have the flute? On the face of it, each of the children has a plausible claim, so arbitrating fairly between them will require negotiation and scrutiny of all the relevant circumstances. In the end, the decision will depend on the relative weight given to the needs of the children and to such matters as artistic expression and relief of poverty.

This story is told by the Indian economist Amartya Sen in *The Idea of Justice* (2009). A decision that is fair and acceptable to all, argues Sen, cannot be reached at the level of principle alone, in the absence of public debate and reasoning. Justice in the abstract may be hard to define, but injustices in the real world are palpable, urgent and often curable, if we engage in public debate and make 'comparisons of actual lives'. 'What moves us is not the realisation that the world falls short of being completely just, which few of us expect, but that there are clearly remediable injustices around us which we want to eliminate.'

differences be disregarded. People should be treated equally *unless* there are good reasons for not doing so. The problem is to decide which differences are relevant.

It might seem reasonable, in determining a just distribution of society's good and bad things, to disregard any differences that people cannot control. I cannot change the colour of my skin or the place of my birth, so these factors should be treated as irrelevant. But there are lots of things about my life that are outside my control. Is it just that my greater talent, or superior intelligence, or appetite for hard work bring me a larger share of life's rewards? Or is it the business of a just society to even out the inequalities that would otherwise inevitably arise? Equality may, uncontroversially, be an essential part of justice, but equality of opportunity and of outcome can mean very different things (*see page 97*).

RAWLS ON JUSTICE

The most significant contribution to the debate over justice in the second half of the 20th century was made by the US political philosopher John Rawls. In constructing his theory of social justice, Rawls addresses the issue of what counts as a morally sufficient reason for departing from equal treatment. He argues that people placed behind an imaginary 'veil of ignorance', which conceals all personal interests and allegiances, would endorse what he calls the 'difference principle' in order to safeguard their own future (unknown) interests. According to this principle, inequalities in the distribution of social goods are justified only if they result in society's worst-off members being better off than they would otherwise have been. Tax cuts for the wealthy, for instance, would be justified, and just, provided that they resulted in an improvement in the fortunes of the least well off.

Although Rawls himself was essentially egalitarian in his outlook, his difference principle can clearly be used to justify very large disparities between the least and most advantaged members of society. His conception of social justice remains the focus of debate and criticism, both positive and negative.

The condensed idea
The crowning glory
of the virtues

24 Equality

Moral questions are typically controversial. On issues such as abortion and homosexuality, for instance, attitudes may have changed dramatically over the past century, but opinions remain divided and debate is often heated. With equality, however, things are rather different. There are few votes for politicians standing up and making the case for inequality – explicitly, at least. As an ideal, equality is all but sacrosanct, readily assumed to be an essential component of a just society.

In the current climate, in Western countries at least, the more obvious forms of inequality, including discrimination on the grounds of race, sex or disability, are no longer acceptable, socially or politically. Prejudices of this kind still persist in people's minds, of course, but they cannot usually be paraded in public without censure. Indeed, equality is now so well established as a principle of ordinary morality that it is easy to forget the extent to which its appeal is modern and its realization imperfect. In reality, the idea that all human beings are (created) equal would have seemed nonsensical, and clearly false, to almost everyone for most of human history.

EQUALITY AS AN ENLIGHTENMENT IDEAL
It is only in the past 350 years, since the Enlightenment, that equality has been elevated to its current position as a cornerstone of political and social thinking. The idealized equality promoted by the English philosopher John Locke was in many respects a secularly inspired reaction to the so-called 'equality before God' that had dominated human affairs over the preceding

TIMELINE

1690	1776	1789
John Locke's *Two Treatises of Government* is published	Inalienable human rights are proclaimed in the US Declaration of Independence	*Declaration of the Rights of Man and of the Citizen* is issued by the French revolutionaries

millennia. The idea that all men (and women) were equal in the eyes of God not only did not preclude vast inequalities between people on Earth but was actually used to justify them.

A hundred years later, in 1776, in drafting the words of the US Declaration of Independence, Thomas Jefferson sanctified the idea that there are certain natural and inalienable rights, including 'Life, Liberty and the pursuit of Happiness', that belong to *all* men and to all men *equally*. Thirteen years later this same ideal became the inspiration for the *Declaration of the Rights of Man and of the Citizen* issued by the French revolutionaries; and with it came their rallying cry: 'Liberty, Equality, Fraternity.'

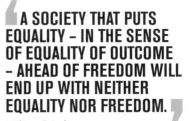

A SOCIETY THAT PUTS EQUALITY – IN THE SENSE OF EQUALITY OF OUTCOME – AHEAD OF FREEDOM WILL END UP WITH NEITHER EQUALITY NOR FREEDOM.

Milton Friedman,
US economist, 1980

CONFLICT OF OPPORTUNITY AND OUTCOME

Locke and Jefferson think of equality in terms of equal rights – most importantly, the right of the individual to live his or her life free from oppression and interference from others (including the state). Such a conception – a classically liberal view – coincides in certain respects with what is now usually called 'equality of opportunity'. This requires that everybody is equal before the law and that no artificial obstacles, such as birth, race or gender, are allowed to stand in the way of people making the most of their natural gifts. Problematically, this idea of equality is actually in conflict with another important conception: equality of outcome (or condition), in which everyone occupies a similar position in terms of wealth, status and other social 'goods'.

Obviously, no two people are the same – everyone is very different in their talents and abilities. So inevitably, if everybody is treated equally and the same opportunities are open to all, some will make more of those opportunities

1989

Communist regimes collapse
in the Soviet Union and
Eastern Europe

2007

Free-market capitalism
is battered by a global
'credit crunch'

All animals are equal ...

In both literature and political thought, equality has been recognized as an ideal in principle, even as its unattainability in reality is lamented. In Anthony Trollope's *The Prime Minister* (1876), the duke of Omnium (the prime minister of the title) bemoans the fact that 'a good word signifying a grand idea has been driven out of the vocabulary of good men. Equality would be a heaven, if we could attain it.' In *Animal Farm* (1945), George Orwell's tyrannical pigs cynically proclaim that 'All animals are equal but some animals are more equal than others', while in the same author's *Nineteen Eighty-Four* (1949), the mysterious Trotsky-like figure Emmanuel Goldstein observes that 'no advance in wealth, no softening of manners, nor reform or revolution has ever brought human equality a millimetre nearer'. Among philosophers there has never been any consensus over the possibility or desirability of equality. Plato reflects a common view among his Greek contemporaries as he derides democracy as a 'charming form of government' that dispenses 'equality to equals and unequals alike'. And to Friedrich Nietzsche, lauding his heroic *Übermensch* ('superman') driven by the will to power to rise above the shackled masses, the very idea of equality is loathsome: 'The doctrine of equality! ... there exists no more poisonous poison: for it *seems* to be preached by justice itself, while it is the *termination* of justice.'

than others and end up in different social and economic situations. Conversely, the only way to ensure that people have equal standing in life is to treat them differently: to give extra help to those who are less talented, more vulnerable, etc.

LIBERAL AND SOCIALIST STATES

These two different ideas of what equality means lead to two different ideas of how a just state should behave. For the liberal, the state's role is to provide a framework of equal rights and liberties that ensures that opportunities are open to all equally; but it has no business to interfere thereafter, in an attempt to even out the inequalities that are bound to emerge in such a system. It is, in effect, an aristocracy of merit, in which elites form on the basis not of birth or wealth but of talent and accomplishment. The liberal state, then, is required to provide a level playing field, but it does not pretend that all players are equally gifted or try to ensure that they are equally rewarded in the exercise of their talents.

The opposing view, usually associated with socialism, assumes that playing fields are never level – they have to be created and tended. The liberal state's minimal intervention is seen as totally inadequate to allow genuine equality to emerge. There are always numerous factors that limit the *effective* liberty that people have to fulfil themselves: for instance, deprived upbringing, poor education and lack of welfare provision. For people really to be equal, public systems of education and welfare must be provided, poverty must be relieved through redistributive taxation, and so on. The just state is one in which true equality – that is, equality of condition – is achieved by allocating resources on the basis of need rather than merit.

EQUALITY AT WAR

It is hardly an exaggeration to say that the second half of the 20th century was an ideological battle between these two different views of equality: between communist regimes, supposedly inspired by Karl Marx's maxim 'to each according to his need', and liberal regimes, supposedly buttressed by the values of free-market capitalism. The widespread failure of communism and its collapse after 1989 suggested, for a while, that the battle was over. But any triumphalism was short-lived, dampened by the traumas to global capitalism in the decades that followed. In the economically chastened world of the early 21st century, grotesque inequalities persist, both within and between countries, but there is little agreement on how best to move forward.

The condensed idea
The cornerstone of justice

25 Tolerance

Is it good to allow other people to do and think things with which you disagree? Or things of which you actually disapprove? If tolerance is a virtue, it ought to be a good thing. But surely the answer depends on what other people are doing and thinking, and perhaps on the basis of your disagreement or disapproval? Seen as a virtue, then, tolerance seems somewhat puzzling.

In fact, the idea of tolerance lies on a major ideological fault line. On one side of the divide, tolerance is the Enlightenment virtue *par excellence*, epitomized in Voltaire's famous remark: 'I disapprove of what you say, but I will defend to the death your right to say it.' Liberal multicultural societies could not survive without tolerance as their guiding light. It ensures that the citizens of such societies are autonomous and open-minded, enjoying rights that guarantee that they are free to hold their own views and allow others to do the same.

At least, this is the picture painted by liberal supporters of such societies. To critics of liberalism, these same things look very different. A non-Western view – one that attaches great importance to traditional beliefs and scriptural values – may see tolerance as mere indulgence, permissiveness as mere licence. Respect for other values, say these critics, quickly slides into respect for all and any values – a kind of decadent and rudderless moral relativism.

THE PARADOX OF TOLERANCE

The ambivalence that surrounds the concept of tolerance is sometimes presented as a paradox. Part of the meaning of tolerance is the idea that

TIMELINE

1689

John Locke's *Letter Concerning Toleration* argues for separation of Church and state

1764

The Enlightenment view of tolerance is given in Voltaire's *Philosophical Dictionary*

you put up with things of which you disapprove, in situations where you can do something about it but choose not to. The degree of tolerance required is proportionate to the level of disapproval: you need to display a high degree of tolerance to restrain yourself from intervening in something that you find highly distasteful. So it is good, apparently, to let bad things happen; and the worse they are, the better it is.

THINK FOR YOURSELVES AND LET OTHERS ENJOY THE PRIVILEGE TO DO SO TOO.

Voltaire,
Treatise on Tolerance, 1763

This paradoxical conclusion becomes even odder if tolerance is considered a virtue (as it often is) and the things that are allowed to happen are seen as morally wrong or bad. On this reading, it is virtuous – it is morally good – to let something morally bad happen; and the worse it is, the greater the virtue displayed. But how, morally, can it be good to let a bad thing happen? If you can stop it (which by definition you can), surely you should?

THE LIBERAL SOLUTION

The liberal response to this paradox has taken two forms. The first is elegantly sketched by Voltaire at the end of the article on tolerance in his *Philosophical Dictionary* (1764):

> We ought to be tolerant of one another, because we are all weak, inconsistent, liable to fickleness and error. Shall a reed laid low in the mud by the wind say to a fellow reed fallen in the opposite direction: 'Crawl as I crawl, wretch, or I shall petition that you be torn up by the roots and burned'?

If tolerance is a virtue, human fallibility may seem a flimsy foundation for it. More influential, in the liberal tradition, is the defence made by John Stuart Mill in his essay *On Liberty* (1859). He argues that:

1859

John Stuart Mill's *On Liberty* argues for tolerance in light of human autonomy

1995

UNESCO issues the Declaration of Principles on Tolerance

UNESCO on tolerance

In 1995 the United Nations Educational, Scientific and Cultural Organization (UNESCO) issued the Declaration of Principles on Tolerance, recognizing this ideal as the guiding principle in the establishment of global peace and harmony. It extols tolerance as 'harmony in difference ... the virtue that makes peace possible [and] contributes to the replacement of the culture of war by a culture of peace ... the responsibility that upholds human rights, pluralism (including cultural pluralism), democracy and the rule of law'.

[a person's] own mode of laying out his existence is the best, not because it is the best in itself, but because it is his own mode. Human beings are not like sheep; and even sheep are not undistinguishably alike. A man cannot get a coat or a pair of boots to fit him, unless they are either made to his measure, or he has a whole warehouseful to choose from: and is it easier to fit him with a life than with a coat?

Mill has a twofold justification for tolerance. First there is the fact of human diversity, which he regards as inherently valuable. Then there is respect for human autonomy, the capacity that allows individuals to make their own choices in life.

The assumption shared by Mill and Voltaire is that the things we should tolerate are never wrong in an absolute sense. Nobody would suggest that we should be tolerant of, say, murder – something that everybody agrees is wrong. But for the rest, no one is in a position to legislate for others, as Voltaire argues; and we should be left to make our own choices, as Mill suggests. There must be limits to toleration, of course, but in general people should be permitted to do and think what they like, provided that their actions and beliefs do not harm others.

CLASH OF CULTURES

From a religious perspective – at least, from a fundamentalist perspective – the problem with tolerance is that there are things, many things, that are wrong (and right) in an absolute sense. Abortion is absolutely wrong if you are a Roman Catholic; publishing a disrespectful picture of the Prophet Mohammed is absolutely wrong if you are a Muslim. In general, such things are wrong because the holy scriptures, containing the word of God, say so, or are interpreted as saying so. The truth of the scriptures is not a matter of doubt, something that people can choose to believe or not, so there is no question of tolerating those who dissent from it.

Locke and the secular state

A seminal contribution to the debate over religious tolerance is John Locke's *Letter Concerning Toleration* (1689). Locke's main purpose is to 'distinguish exactly the business of civil government from that of religion'. He insists that it is none of the state's business to interfere in the 'care of souls' and that in this area the application of its penalties is 'absolutely impertinent'. The mischief, in Locke's view, lies in the confusion of the functions of Church and state, and his insistence on strictly separating them has provided one of the central pillars of modern liberal society.

This is a fundamentalist view, perhaps, but it is quite consistent with the logic that underlies most religions. Christianity and Islam, for instance, both claim to be the one true faith, and clearly they cannot both be right. These religions are intrinsically antagonistic: the tale of crusades, inquisitions, jihads and fatwahs throughout history is no aberration, and it is no surprise that they are intolerant of one another. The truth is so important that it is not unreasonable, in the logic of their own religion, for faithful followers to see it as their duty to impose their views on others.

The liberal ideal of tolerance embraces the freedom for people to entertain any beliefs, including religious ones, provided that they do not harm others. The inherent antagonism that exists between religions, however, means that orthodox followers of those religions, enjoying such rights and freedoms within a liberal state, are bound to come into conflict. The liberal antidote to this danger is secularism: a clear separation of religion, seen as a matter of private observance, and the state, so allowing a neutral public space where citizens can meet as equals and without prejudice. From a fundamentalist perspective, however, the idea of a purely secular state is no less intolerable than tolerance itself and unlikely to remain unchallenged.

The condensed idea
A paradoxical virtue

26 Rights

How should we be treated? What limits should be set on our behaviour? In answering such questions we usually appeal to the notion of rights: the idea that there are certain good things that people are entitled to have and certain bad things that they can expect to avoid. These various entitlements are often said to be natural – belonging to everyone equally by virtue of the dignity due to them as human beings – but in fact the nature and status of rights are disputed.

Rights are connected to other ethical ideas, such as duties and principles. If killing is wrong, it implies that there is a duty not to kill; people have a right to life. If theft is wrong, it implies that there is a duty not to steal; people have a right to keep what they own – a right to property. In other words, the principles that killing and theft are wrong imply the rights to life and property. A moral system – a system explaining what we should and should not do – can thus be seen as a complex structure of interlocking and overlapping rights.

Today, a bewildering array of rights is recognized or asserted – some ethical, others legal, and yet others social or informal. All of these various rights can be understood in terms of four basic types: privilege, power, immunity and claim.

THE NATURE OF RIGHTS

You have a **privilege** (or **liberty**) right to do something if you are under no obligation not to do it. You have a privilege right to free speech provided that there is no prohibition, legal or other, on your doing so.

TIMELINE

1690	1785
John Locke argues that rights are natural, inalienable and universal	Immanuel Kant's categorical imperative requires that people always be treated as ends

Life, liberty and the pursuit of happiness

The modern origins of human rights (though not the name) are to be found most prominently in the works of the English political theorist John Locke. Writing in the aftermath of England's Glorious Revolution of 1688, Locke argues that human beings are endowed with certain natural rights, which spring from man's essential nature and belong to individuals self-evidently, by virtue of their humanity. For this reason they are inalienable – they cannot be renounced; and universal – they belong to all people equally. The three principal rights named by Locke – life, liberty and property – were famously echoed in Thomas Jefferson's drafting of the US Declaration of Independence (1776), where he asserts as self-evident truths that 'all men are created equal; that they are endowed by their Creator with certain unalienable rights; that among these are life, liberty and the pursuit of happiness'.

You have a **claim** right if a third party is under an obligation to you to do (or to refrain from doing) something. A child has a claim right that her parents give her adequate care and refrain from mistreating her. A claim right implies a corresponding duty, in this case a duty on a child's parents to give adequate care.

You have a **power** right if you are entitled or authorized to change the form of other rights, either your own or other people's. The right to property implies the power right to end that right, by selling or transferring the property to another. The rights to privacy and anonymity imply the power rights to waive those entitlements.

You have an **immunity** right, in respect of a third party, if that third party lacks the power right to change your rights in some way. Under the Fifth Amendment to the US Constitution (1789), a witness cannot be compelled to give evidence that may incriminate herself. This right is an immunity against self-incrimination.

1795
Jeremy Bentham ridicules the idea that rights are natural

1948
The United Nations adopts the Universal Declaration of Human Rights

1977
Ronald Dworkin introduces the idea of rights as trumps

Positive and negative rights

Especially in political contexts, rights are often distinguished as negative or positive. This distinction mirrors that between the negative and positive concepts of freedom (*see page 41*). Your right to do as you please in the privacy of your own home is a negative right, in that it is necessary only that others refrain from interfering with you for the right to be respected. In contrast, unemployment pay and other welfare benefits are positive rights, in that others are required to provide some good or service if those rights are to be upheld.

TRUMP TROUBLE

Rights are generally thought of as having a special force that means they are able to override other considerations: rights are said to be 'trumps' – they have priority over reasons that point to a different course of action. For instance, the right to a fair trial is a sufficient reason that people should not be imprisoned without trial, even if (say) reasons of national security suggest otherwise. Likewise, the right to life requires that one innocent person should not be sacrificed even if many innocent lives would thereby be saved.

In practice, however, matters are not so simple. For one thing, rights conflict and compete. The press's right to freedom of expression, for instance, may infringe an individual's right to privacy. The king of trumps always beats the queen, but one right may trump another in one context but not in another. Real life is messy: the 'public interest' is held to justify, in some cases but not others, the press infringing someone's privacy. Rights may give good grounds for a particular course of action, but the grounds are rarely, if ever, conclusive. The attraction of rights is partly that they seem to offer clear guidance. If they lose this aura of certainty and clarity, some of their appeal is lost with it.

THE BASIS OF RIGHTS

The common view is that rights should be respected, over and above other considerations, because they are fundamental entitlements with which human beings are naturally endowed. Such rights are natural in that they are rooted in essential attributes of our human nature, such as rationality and autonomy. As human beings, we have an inherent dignity: rights are an expression or reflection of our essential value, and to violate those rights is to devalue us.

This understanding of rights, seeing them as entitlements worthy of respect for their own sake, sits most comfortably in the duty-based (deontological) ethical tradition that goes back to Immanuel Kant. His formulation of the categorical imperative that requires that human beings always be treated as ends, never as means, places a similar significance in human dignity (*see page 55*). This approach, which takes its lead from the nature of the right-holder, does not commend itself to consequentialists, who – in the case of rights as elsewhere – insist that we start by looking at outcomes and work our way back to determine the nature of rights. Typically forthright, the pioneer of utilitarianism Jeremy Bentham famously described natural rights as 'simple nonsense ... natural and imprescriptible [inalienable] rights, rhetorical nonsense – nonsense upon stilts'. His view is that a right is 'the child of law', i.e. a matter of human convention. From this perspective, rights are essentially instrumental, justified – like anything else – if they tend to bring about an optimal state of affairs, to be measured (in Bentham's view) in terms of utility, or human happiness.

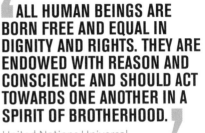

ALL HUMAN BEINGS ARE BORN FREE AND EQUAL IN DIGNITY AND RIGHTS. THEY ARE ENDOWED WITH REASON AND CONSCIENCE AND SHOULD ACT TOWARDS ONE ANOTHER IN A SPIRIT OF BROTHERHOOD.

United Nations Universal Declaration of Human Rights, 1948

THE RIGHTS AND WRONGS OF RIGHTS

Understanding morality in terms of rights shifts attention from actions to agents, as the bearers of rights. Focusing on people and what is due to them has advantages. The human rights movement (in the broadest sense) has its origins in the Enlightenment, when the dignity of man was elevated as never before by philosophers and revolutionaries alike. A common criticism is that focusing on the individual has promoted individualism and neglect of social virtues such as charity and benevolence. Another criticism, related to the first but not entirely consistent with it, is that attending to rights, rather than duties – on what people should get, rather than what they can give – has encouraged a culture of selfishness and dependency.

The condensed idea
Natural endowments –
or nonsense on stilts?

27 Altruism

The idea of altruism – selflessly promoting the good of others, without consideration of one's own interests – has always played a pivotal part in ethics, both religious and philosophical. Altruistic behaviour is seen not only in individuals who benefit others – for example, through acts of generosity, mercy, charity or philanthropy – but also in abstract bodies, including the state, which may be responsible for such benefactions as scholarships, welfare schemes, foreign aid and disaster relief.

In religious ethics, altruism and its close relative benevolence – the disposition to behave altruistically or kindly towards others – have usually been regarded as unequivocally good; they are, for instance, cornerstones of Christian morality. Philosophically, the notion of altruism is somewhat more contentious. For one thing, doubts have been raised about the moral value of philanthropy and charity, in that they imply an inherently unequal relationship between one who has more money (or some other good) than she needs and another who does not have enough; sometimes, therefore, they may serve as a fig-leaf for a broader social imbalance or dysfunction.

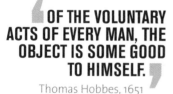

OF THE VOLUNTARY ACTS OF EVERY MAN, THE OBJECT IS SOME GOOD TO HIMSELF.

Thomas Hobbes, 1651

DUTY BOUND?

The extent to which benevolent acts are a matter of duty is also open to question. If justice consists in giving people their due (as Aristotle thought), there seems to be a duty or obligation to behave justly. If benevolence consists in giving people *more* than is strictly due to them, being

A tyranny against nature

One of the most virulent attacks on altruism (and conventional morality in general) was launched by the German philosopher Friedrich Nietzsche towards the end of the 19th century. He regarded benevolence as a 'tyranny against nature' – an inversion or perversion of the natural order. Spurred on by the Christian Church and driven by resentment and jealousy, the weak and the ugly have initiated a 'slave revolt' against the strong and the beautiful. Cowed by morality's weapons of guilt and blame, the best and noblest of humanity unwittingly connive in their own oppression and enslavement, blinded to their true and natural goal – the will to power.

benevolent appears to be beyond the call of duty, or optional, from a moral perspective – a moral ideal, perhaps, but not a duty. Many philosophers take a different view and argue that showing benevolent concern for others is a moral requirement. But if this is so, how much is required? What limit can or should be set on benevolence?

More fundamentally, philosophers have long been divided over whether altruism really exists at all. Several of the ancient Greek sophists – basically, philosophers for hire – who locked horns with Plato's Socrates, glibly assumed that benevolence to others was really a sham and that the true motive, if you scratched beneath the surface, was always self-interest. In more recent times, some philosophers have proposed that people are, as a matter of fact, motivated only by concern for their own interests (psychological egoism). A few, including Friedrich Nietzsche in the 19th century and

MEN OFTEN ACT KNOWINGLY AGAINST THEIR INTEREST.

David Hume, 1740

Ayn Rand in the 20th, have explicitly rejected altruism and endorsed some kind of ethical egoism – the view that people ought to do what is in their own self-interest.

1859

Charles Darwin explains evolution by natural selection in the *Origin of Species*

1887–8

Friedrich Nietzsche attacks altruism's role in emasculating the true self

1964

Ayn Rand argues for ethical egoism, the 'virtue of selfishness'

Biological altruism and kin selection

Since the revolutionary work of Charles Darwin, philosophical doubts about altruism have been reinforced by biological ones. The key to Darwinian evolution is survival of the fittest – roughly, individuals who have (heritable) qualities that allow them to survive longer generally produce more offspring and pass on more of these qualities to the next generation. Given such a mechanism, how can a disposition to put others' interests before one's own possibly survive? Evolutionary theory has an answer: kin selection. It turns out that it is not the survival of an altruistic *individual* that matters, but the survival of the genetic *material* that contributed to its altruistic disposition – and this can be achieved through offspring and other relatives who share some of the same genes. This explains why some species of deer and monkey, for instance, give warning signals that a predator is nearby, even though they risk danger to themselves by doing so. It may also partly explain how altruistic behaviour evolved in humans. The problem, though, is that biological altruism of this kind is not 'real' altruism at all: it still involves the agent's (ultimate) self-interest – or at least its genes' interest.

CAN WE BE SELFLESSLY GOOD TO OTHERS?

There is an informal line of argument that is commonly used to show that any (apparently) altruistic act is only ever done from self-interest. If you help someone by giving them ten pounds, you are evidently motivated to help them – you must, in some sense, *want* to help them; and in helping them, you clearly satisfy that want. But if you act in such a way that you satisfy your own want, surely you must be acting in your own interest, not out of consideration for others? Following this line of argument, it is suggested that every action is self-interested, and hence that psychological egoism is true and altruism impossible – by definition.

Chief among the deficiencies of this argument is an inadequate understanding of motivation. Even if both agents are motivated by self-interest (in this attenuated sense), we clearly wish to distinguish between one who gives ten pounds in the expectation of getting nothing in return (except, perhaps, having his want satisfied) and another who does so in the expectation of having his lawn mown (as well, perhaps, as his want satisfied). It may be impossible, in the end, to know for certain what motivates people – what 'makes them tick' – but we can surely make a better guess if we look beyond the meaning of words to how things actually are in the world.

The political theorist Thomas Hobbes is often cited as a psychological egoist because he assumes that people in the 'state of nature' (that is, before the advent of the state) are essentially self-interested, concerned only to preserve their own skins (*see page 77*). His view is that human beings are *basically* individualistic, living cooperatively in society only because that is the surest means of surviving. There is, however, much empirical evidence on the other side – from science and from our own eyes – to suggest that we are in fact essentially *social* animals. Certainty may not be appropriate in such matters, but we are perhaps more likely to agree with the Scottish philosopher David Hume, who argued against Hobbes that, 'The voice of nature and experience seems plainly to oppose the selfish theory.'

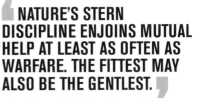

NATURE'S STERN DISCIPLINE ENJOINS MUTUAL HELP AT LEAST AS OFTEN AS WARFARE. THE FITTEST MAY ALSO BE THE GENTLEST.

Theodosius Dobzhansky, 1962

The condensed idea
Benevolence:
selfless or selfish?

28 Friendship

'No one would choose to have every good thing there is if he had to enjoy it alone,' observed Aristotle, 'because man is a political being and it is his nature to live with others. Even the happy man, therefore, lives with others, for he has everything that is naturally good. And clearly it is better to spend time with friends and good men than with strangers or chance acquaintances. Therefore the happy man needs friends.'

In the *Nicomachean Ethics* the Greek philosopher Aristotle argues that friendship is a vital component of the good life. Quoting the popular saying 'When fortune smiles, what need is there of friends?', he challenges the view that friends are needed only in times of adversity. Quite the contrary: they are among the greatest of goods that help man on the path to self-knowledge and *eudaimonia*, the state of 'happiness' – flourishing and well-being – that is the proper aim of human activity.

AN ANTIDOTE TO EGOISM

Aristotle's claim that a friend is 'another self' has influenced much subsequent analysis of friendship. While some so-called friendships are

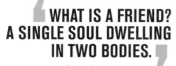

WHAT IS A FRIEND? A SINGLE SOUL DWELLING IN TWO BODIES.
Aristotle, 4th century BC

made for pleasure or gain, friendship proper is variously described as a bond between individuals, a union of minds, even a shared identity, in which each wishes for the other as he does for himself. Like-mindedness in interests and values may sow the seeds of friendship, but that sympathy of outlook is dynamic, gradually enriching the character of each friend as the relationship matures.

TIMELINE

4th century BC	4th century BC
Aristotle explores the idea of friendship in the *Nicomachean Ethics*	Aristotle, in the *Magna Moralia* (attributed), compares friendship to a mirror

The mirror of the soul

In the *Magna Moralia* (a treatise attributed to Aristotle that summarizes his ethical views), Aristotle famously compares friendship to a mirror to explain its role in shaping a person's moral development. My knowledge of my own character is necessarily limited and imperfect. So – to the extent that friendship depends on similarity of character – a friend can serve as a mirror into my own soul, allowing me to get a fuller, more truthful view of myself. In this way friendship promotes the self-knowledge that is essential if an individual is to attain *eudaimonia* – the happiness, or human flourishing, that is the greatest good and culmination of philosophy.

The crucial aspect of true friendship, for Aristotle and others, is that it necessarily embodies a concern for another's good that is similar to one's own. We come to love our friends much as we love ourselves, and to wish what is best for them, purely for their own sake. This selfless concern for the well-being of another, so central to the experience of friendship, is a strong antidote to the view, shared by philosophers and ordinary people alike, that the prime motivation behind human activity is egoism – that everything we do is done, ultimately, in our own interest. Friendship, instead, supports the idea that humans are naturally altruistic and social beings (*see chapter 27*).

A FLY IN THE OINTMENT OF ETHICAL THEORY

Another aspect of friendship is that friends can look to one another for support. In this respect they are similar to members of a family. It is usually unspoken, but there is a trust, an expectation, that a friend (or a family member) will be there to help in times of need, great or small. You might, for instance, help out a friend on a charity walk, even if you are not at all sympathetic to the

1998

Winnie the Pooh is declared the world's ambassador of friendship

Man's best friend?

We can certainly love our pets – but love is often unrequited. Can we really be *friends* with the dogs, cats, hamsters, snakes, goldfish and other animals that we take into our homes as companions? Many people treat them as members of the family and would not question the obligation to feed them and provide for their needs. But if friendship implies a reciprocity of feeling and a mingling of minds, can these lovable lodgers truly be friends? And if they are not our friends, can we justify the special obligations that we feel towards them? Should we be spending many billions on pet food and medication – not to mention all-weather dog-boots – when there are many millions of our own species in desperate need of these same things (well, perhaps not the dog-boots)? Animals and humans, friends and strangers: these issues highlight the extent to which our moral priorities in relation to our fellow creatures are confused and inconsistent.

charitable aim. So, when asked why you agreed to raise money to buy dog-boots for strays, you will say that you did it 'out of friendship'. The reason that you did what you did – and felt that you *should* do what you did – was not that the cause was good, or that stray dogs shouldn't get cold feet; the *only* motivation, in this case, was your relationship to the person who asked you to do it.

THE GOOD MAN IS RELATED TO HIS FRIEND AS HE IS TO HIMSELF, FOR HIS FRIEND IS ANOTHER SELF.

Aristotle, *Nicomachean Ethics*, 4th century BC

In other words, we expect people to favour their friends (and family), to show partiality towards them. Common sense suggests that there are special obligations owed to friends, duties based on personal considerations. But this is problematic for ethical theory, which tends to prioritize the universal over the particular or personal. The consequentialist (utilitarian or other) says that we should do whatever brings about the best state of affairs (where 'best' means the largest net gain in utility, happiness, etc.); a deontologist, advocating a morality based on duty, insists that there are certain things we should do because they are right in themselves. Neither approach is consistent with the kind of concern, partial and personal, that is apparently an essential element of friendship.

So, it seems either that these theories are deficient in some way, or that the common view that there are certain things we should do for friends *because* they are friends is unfounded. At the very least, if the theories are sound, it must mean that the duties of friendship are not *moral* duties; and where the demands of friendship and morality clash, as inevitably they will, it must mean that the former are in some sense *im*moral.

There are doubtless situations where people favour their friends when they should not; even where parents favour their children when they should not. Still, it is unsettling that ethical theory is not better able to accommodate the kind of personal considerations that motivate us to do much of what we do. Aspects of friendship suggest that the tendency of theorists to focus on actions rather than agents – to attend to what we should do rather than who is doing it – may lead to a skewed picture of morality.

The condensed idea
Does friendship make us do wrong?

Heroes and saints

A squad of soldiers is engaged in a training exercise using live hand grenades. Suddenly a grenade slips from the hand of one of the soldiers, endangering the lives of all the men. One of their number thereupon throws himself over the loose grenade, absorbing the explosion with his own body and so sacrificing his life to save his colleagues.

What are we to make of the soldier's behaviour? If he had not thrown himself on the grenade, we would hardly say that he had failed in his duty – that he had acted wrongly in some way. Nor would we blame any of the other soldiers for not trying to be the one to sacrifice himself. Rather, we would single out the man for special praise. If our duty is what we should do and are expected to do, his act of bravery went *beyond* the call of duty: we admire him for doing what he did but would not have blamed him had he acted differently.

SUPEREROGATORY ACTS

It seems quite natural to view morality as operating on two levels. On one level, there are things we are all morally required to do: basic obligations that are a matter of duty and set the minimum standard of ordinary morality. Often these are stated negatively, as obligations that we are wrong not to meet: we ought not to steal and we ought not to kill. We are expected to meet these obligations ourselves and expect others to do likewise.

TIMELINE

1785	18th–19th century
Immanuel Kant asserts the supreme value of moral agency in *Groundwork of the Metaphysics of Morals*	Foundations of classical utilitarianism are set forth by Jeremy Bentham and John Stuart Mill

Counsels of perfection

Christianity has a complex relationship with 'acts of supererogation' – acts whose performance goes beyond what is required by God. In the Gospel of Matthew, a rich young man asks Jesus what he must do to gain eternal life. Jesus tells him to obey God's commandments; when he replies that he already observes them, Jesus says: 'If you want to be perfect, go, sell your possessions and give to the poor, and you will have treasure in heaven.' According to Christian teaching, voluntary poverty (together with chastity and obedience) is one of the three 'counsels of perfection' – conditions that are not required but which help to free the soul from worldly distractions. Why, then, is it not the duty of Christians to obey these counsels, if they are thereby brought closer to God? The answer seems to be surprisingly pragmatic: not all Christians are strong enough to follow such exalted paths, and each is expected to find his own way to God. On a practical level, it is easy to see why leaders of the early Church were anxious not to make universal chastity a requirement.

In addition to these ordinary moral duties, there are, at a more elevated level, moral ideals. These are often expressed positively and may be open-ended: thus, while there are ordinary duties not to steal and kill, great generosity is an ideal that is in principle unlimited. Such behaviour goes beyond what is required by ordinary morality and falls into a category of so-called 'supererogatory acts' – acts that are praiseworthy to perform but not blameworthy to omit. These acts are the province of heroes and saints. Such people may have ideals that require them to act in a certain way, and they (and they alone) may blame themselves if they fail to live up to them. But such ideals are essentially self-imposed, determining a *personal* sense of duty that cannot reasonably be expected of others.

1958

The story of the brave soldier and the grenade is told by the British philosopher J. O. Urmson

CAN DOING GOOD BE OPTIONAL?

From a theoretical perspective, the idea that there are good acts that are not obligatory may appear problematic. Theories about how we should understand morality are typically based on some conception of what is good; what is right and what is wrong are then defined by reference to this standard. But if something manifestly meets – indeed, surpasses – this standard, how can it be that it is not required that we do it?

THE ORDINARY MAN IS INVOLVED IN ACTION, THE HERO ACTS.

Henry Miller,
American writer, 1952

According to classical utilitarianism, an action is good if it increases general utility (happiness, according to Bentham and Mill), and the best action in any situation is the one that produces the most utility. But if doing the right thing is to produce as much utility as possible, then there is only ever one right course of action – namely, the one that maximizes utility. This is what you should do, even if that means spending every minute serving others, giving every last penny you can spare to relieve poverty, neglecting your own immediate concerns (including your family) – provided, in each case, that you thereby maximize utility overall. For the utilitarian, it seems, there are no such things as supererogatory acts.

GETTING PERSONAL

There are committed utilitarians today who accept this conclusion. They deny that it is ever permissible, in any given situation, not to do the best thing (that is, the thing that maximizes utility) and urge that we alter our ways of life accordingly. There have always been saints, of course, literal and metaphorical, who have given up everything to dedicate their lives to do what they feel is right. But any ethical theory that *requires* us to behave in such ways is bound to mark most of us down as moral failures. That doesn't make the theory wrong, but it does make it look highly idealistic.

More pragmatic theorists attempt to explain or play down the apparent conflict with ordinary morality. One strategy is to appeal to some form of exemption or mitigation that excuses a person from performing an action that would otherwise be obligatory. In the grenade case, for instance, we might excuse any one soldier from sacrificing himself simply because of the personal danger involved. It would be immoral not to stretch out an arm to fish out a child drowning in a pond, but we would take a different view of someone who did not swim out in a stormy sea to do so. Or I might excuse myself from the obligation to give away my wealth in order to relieve poverty on the grounds that I have personal commitments such as children of my own to support.

In real life we appeal to such mitigating factors all the time. The problem is that the introduction of *personal* considerations of this kind is bound to conflict with the ideas of impartiality and universality that are central to most ethical theories. This can cut either way, of course: if the conflict is real and demands that we reform either 'ordinary' morality (our commonsense intuitions and the like) or moral theory, most people would say that the latter should give way. Again, it doesn't make most people right, but there are several philosophers, too, who think that the failure of utilitarianism, in particular, to take sufficient account of personal considerations and commitments seriously undermines its credibility (*see chapter 30*).

The condensed idea
Beyond the call of duty

30 Integrity

George is a trained chemist, desperately in need of a job to support his young family. A well-paid position comes up in a laboratory dedicated to research into biological and chemical weapons. But George is a committed pacifist, deeply opposed to such research. He is offered the job and finds out at the same time that, if he declines the position, it will be taken by another candidate who is sure to pursue the work with much greater vigour than he. Should he take the job?

Different moral theories may reach different conclusions on this question. The utilitarian verdict will probably be that George should take the job: his conscientious objections have to be weighed in the balance of general utility against the welfare of his family, the potential harm that the other candidate may bring about, and so on. A Kantian, on the other hand, might argue that the absolute prohibition on killing, or assisting in killing, is what matters here and that no amount of good consequences should count against this.

The author of this story, the English philosopher Bernard Williams, is not much concerned with the *result* of George's deliberations – whether this or that system issues the 'right' answer in this case. His concern is with the nature of moral theories themselves and their ambition to systematize our moral lives: supposedly to discover – in fact, to invent – a neat and self-contained structure in which principles are invoked and rules are applied in order to resolve moral dilemmas. Such theories underplay, or ignore

TIMELINE

1785	18th–19th century
Immanuel Kant sets forth his moral theory in *Groundwork of the Metaphysics of Morals*	The foundations of utilitarianism are laid down by Jeremy Bentham and John Stuart Mill

altogether, the significance of moral agency, failing to capture the essential relationship between a moral agent such as George and his actions. In the case of George, they fail to acknowledge the extent to which his moral identity is determined by personal commitments or 'ground projects', such as his pacifism. These are, essentially, the things that make George George and give meaning to his life; failure to take proper account of them in his moral decision-making effectively undermines his 'integrity' – literally, his 'wholeness' as a moral agent.

A VIEW FROM NOWHERE

Williams's central objection is to the notion of impartiality that lies at the heart of ethical systems such as Kantianism and utilitarianism. This is not the familiar and unexceptionable impartiality that requires that we do not allow our moral judgments to become clouded or distorted by irrelevant bias or prejudice. Rather, the problem for supporters of some or other ethical theory is that, in seeking systematically to avoid the bias of the individual perspective, they insist on adopting a perspective that is really no perspective at all. The Victorian philosopher Henry Sidgwick, for instance, proposes that the utilitarian should assume the 'point of view of the universe'. But what, we may wonder, can it possibly mean to see things from such a perspective?

> **IT CANNOT BE A REASONABLE AIM THAT I ... SHOULD TAKE AS THE IDEAL VIEW OF THE WORLD ... A VIEW FROM NO POINT OF VIEW AT ALL.**
> Bernard Williams,
> *Making Sense of Humanity*, 1995

It is simply absurd, Williams argues, in the area of *practical* decision-making – in deciding what I ought to *do* – to make it a condition of any procedure that I disregard the very fact that the perspective involved happens to be my own. The business of morality is *essentially* first-personal: to ask a moral agent to 'rise above' the personal perspective – to ignore, in effect, that a given action is her action, a necessary part of her life story – is profoundly to misunderstand

1874

Henry Sidgwick expounds his utilitarian philosophy in *The Method of Ethics*

1973

Bernard Williams tells the stories of George and Jim in *Utilitarianism: For and Against*

Jim and the Indians

Another famous case used by Bernard Williams is the story of the botanist Jim, who finds himself in the central square of a small South American town. Here, a group of twenty natives, randomly selected, have been lined up against a wall and are about to be shot in order to dissuade others from rebellion. As an honoured visitor, Jim is offered the privilege of shooting one of the Indians himself, in which case the others will be spared. If he refuses, the execution will proceed as previously planned. What should Jim do? As in the case of George, the point is not that utilitarianism comes up with the wrong answer; indeed, in this case, Williams supposes that Jim probably should shoot the Indian, as the utilitarian suggests. The real problem lies in the way that the answer is reached: 'It is ... a question of what sort of considerations come into finding the answer.' Certainly, the pangs of conscience that would haunt a man put in Jim's wretched predicament, the agony of regret and self-recrimination that would live with him forever afterwards, are quite lost in the crude balance-sheet of utilitarian calculation.

the nature of agency. The idea of 'impartial agency' is nonsense, Williams suggests, and in supposing otherwise utilitarianism fails to recognize the intrinsic separateness of individuals.

It is due to this faulty notion of impartiality that utilitarianism gives an inadequate (at best) account of cases such as George's. Suppose, for further example, that a house is on fire; in one room your two children are trapped, in another there are three children you don't know. You only have time to rescue the children from one room. The 'point of view of the universe' makes no allowance for relationships that are peculiar to you, so, in this case, apparently, you are required to save the three strangers. The utilitarian may protest that personal commitments are themselves a source of utility and so may have a place in her world, yet this does little to dispel the suspicion that such commitments have not only been undervalued but basically misconstrued.

ASKING TOO MUCH

A further (and related) problem typical of ethical theories is their tendency to simplify through generalization. In order to streamline what is essentially complex, such theories may seek to systematize by taking on a quasi-legal aspect – looking to support a particular moral obligation by invoking a more general obligation, of which the case in hand is supposedly explained as an instance. In the case of utilitarianism, wholesale application of the standard of utility leads to a kind of generalized accountability where we are no less responsible for what we do not do than for what we do. If I choose to play football on a Saturday afternoon rather than raise money for charity, I may find that I have blood on my hands, as the result of my choice may be a number of famine deaths for which I am morally accountable. The realm of the morally indifferent – of the many things that are not normally thought to have any moral significance – may shrink dramatically, and we may soon find ourselves required *not* to do anything we are not *required* to do. Our overburdened consciences may urge us to reform our lives completely. The utilitarian may welcome such a development – nobody said morality was easy – but for most of us such demands are almost certain to end in failure.

INTEGRITY HAS NO NEED OF RULES.
Albert Camus,
The Myth of Sisyphus, 1942

The condensed idea
Agent-centred morality

31 Crime and punishment

Crime is 'the measure of a State's failure, all crime in the end is the crime of the community'. So wrote the English author H. G. Wells, in his guise as social commentator, in the first decade of the 20th century. Wells reflects a common view that one of the central purposes of the state is to maintain social order by ensuring that the laws assented to by society as a whole are obeyed. Crime, which violates such laws, disrupts social order and is the clearest challenge to the state's authority. The legitimacy of the state thus depends on its ability to prevent crime.

Punishing those who break its laws is one of the principal ways in which the state seeks to combat crime. Yet seen from another perspective, the institution of punishment is puzzling. The state's normal duty is to defend the rights of its citizens – to protect them from harm, to guarantee their freedom of movement, to allow them full political expression. Only in the context of its penal activities does the state think it appropriate to inflict harm on its members – to restrict their liberty to move and speak freely, perhaps even to deprive them of their lives. These two functions of the state – to protect and to punish – appear to be necessary and yet to conflict with one another.

Some find the institutionalized use of punishment in what is claimed to be civilized society indefensible. It is as if the state stoops to the level of the criminal in the very act of punishing him. Oscar Wilde, for one, wrote in 1891 that society is 'infinitely more brutalized by the habitual employment of

TIMELINE

7th century BC	1789
Draco establishes a famously harsh legal code in ancient Athens	The utilitarian Jeremy Bentham argues that punishment is a necessary evil

punishment than it is by the occasional occurrence of crime'. How, then, is it morally justified for the state to inflict harm on its citizens in the form of punishment?

A NECESSARY EVIL ...

One important view, often labelled 'liberal', is practical and utilitarian: punishment is a necessary evil, justified because the social benefits it brings outweigh the suffering it causes. 'All punishment is mischief,' insisted the English philosopher Jeremy Bentham, 'all punishment in itself is evil.' One obvious benefit is that the danger to the public posed by murderers and other serious offenders is reduced by their imprisonment. Another benefit claimed for punishment is its deterrent value, though here the case is less easy to make. As a matter of justice, it is questionable whether it is fair to punish people, not (or not solely) for the crimes they have committed, but in order to deter others from committing crimes. On a practical level, there are also doubts over the effectiveness of deterrence, as there is evidence that it is not so much punishment as fear of capture that deters would-be criminals.

Perhaps the most compelling argument in favour of punishment, at least from the liberal perspective, is the hope of rehabilitating offenders – of reforming and re-educating them in such a way that they can become full and useful members of society. Here, too, however, there are practical doubts over the ability of penal systems – most current systems, at any rate – to deliver this kind of benign outcome.

... OR JUST DESERTS?

The other major tradition holds that punishment is justified as retribution; as such, it is good in itself, irrespective of the benefits it may bring. Everybody is under an obligation to abide by society's rules, so those who choose not to do so incur a penalty (a debt or due) that must be paid. A minor offender

1891

Oscar Wilde's *The Soul of Man under Socialism* suggests that punishment is worse than the disease it is supposed to cure

1905

H. G. Wells's *A Modern Utopia* asserts that crime is a reflection of social failure

The draconian route to road safety

Asked why he prescribed the death penalty even for minor offences, the Athenian lawgiver Draco is supposed to have said that the lesser crimes deserved it and he couldn't think of any harsher punishment for the greater ones. Such 'draconian' justice seems to conflict with the view of punishment as retribution, because the punishment doesn't fit the crime. Paying with your life for breaking the speed limit seems unjust, because it is entirely disproportionate: retributive justice demands that you get the punishment you deserve – you should pay your debt to society, nothing more and nothing less. From a utilitarian perspective, however, things look rather different. If punishment is a necessary evil, the principal aim should be to get the most benefit (in terms of deterrence, public protection, etc.) at the smallest cost in suffering (on the part of those who are punished). So how many people would risk speeding in Draco's Athens? If the laws are so harsh that no one dares to break them, the public will be perfectly protected, every would-be criminal completely deterred: a crime-free utopia – and safe roads – at the cost of manifest injustice.

may literally 'repay his debt' to society, by paying a fine, while in more serious cases a greater price must be paid, in loss of liberty or (in some jurisdictions) loss of life. The basic idea here is that justice requires that people should get what they deserve; in both cases, punishment is deserved and some kind of balance is restored by its imposition.

More radically, there is a widely held view that 'the punishment should fit the crime'. This is sometimes taken to imply that crime and punishment should be equivalent not only in severity but also in kind. Defenders of the death penalty, for instance, often argue that the only proper reparation for the taking of life is the loss of life (*see page 128*). The point is less persuasive in the case of some other crimes, and few would suggest that blackmailers, for instance, should be blackmailed. The chief difficulty in this approach is to keep a sanitary distance between (supposedly moral) retribution and (morally indefensible) revenge. It may be objected that punishment expresses society's disgust or outrage at a particular act, but when retribution is stripped down to little more than an urge for vengeance, it scarcely appears adequate as a justification for punishment.

AN UNEASY COMPROMISE

It is often easy to pick holes in any particular analysis of punishment – to show its inadequacy by citing counter-examples where an offender does not present a danger to the public or does not need reform, or whose punishment would not have any deterrent value. For this reason, justifications of punishment and penal policy tend to take a scattergun approach and are based not only on matters of principle but on more mundane practical considerations: what is claimed to work in fact is used to defend what is said to be right in principle. Several recent theorists have adopted this approach, presenting hybrid accounts of punishment that combine utilitarian and retributivist elements. Such an analysis probably *describes* quite accurately what most people think about punishment; whether it fully explains or justifies it is less clear.

> **THE IDEA OF JUSTICE MUST BE SACRED IN ANY GOOD SOCIETY ... CRIME AND BAD LIVES ARE THE MEASURE OF A STATE'S FAILURE, ALL CRIME IN THE END IS THE CRIME OF THE COMMUNITY.**
>
> H. G. Wells,
> *A Modern Utopia*, 1905

The condensed idea
Righteous anger or necessary evil?

The death penalty

As a result of decisions made in courts of law, the lives of thousands of people are ended each year by a range of means, ancient and modern, that includes electrocution, hanging, gassing, beheading, stoning, shooting and lethal injection. Worldwide, the number of judicial executions has been declining, but capital punishment is still actively used in over 50 countries. The undisputed execution capital of the world is China, where it is estimated that several thousand people are put to death each year – more than the rest of the world put together.

Capital punishment is an enormously divisive issue, and justifications of its use are rarely simple. Proponents may feel that killing killers, for instance, is the morally right thing to do, but they almost invariably back up their argument by suggesting that the use of such punishment has good social consequences. In a similar vein, opponents of the death penalty usually claim both that it is wrong in itself and that it either fails to deliver the benefits claimed for it or that its effects are actually damaging.

PAYING THE ULTIMATE PRICE

The idea that the death penalty is good in itself reflects an essentially retributive conception of justice. Law and morality depend on the fact that people are accountable for their actions, and they should pay a price for what they have done. For the most serious crimes, therefore – usually murder but sometimes other offences as well – it is right that the wrongdoer pays the ultimate price of his own life. Sometimes religious doctrine is used to support

TIMELINE

1964	1965	1969
The last execution takes place in the UK	Moors murderer Ian Brady is arrested and subsequently convicted and sentenced to life imprisonment	Ernest van den Haag argues that the death penalty is the 'best bet', given the uncertainty of its deterrent effect

the retributive case. The so-called *lex talionis* (law of retaliation) of the Hebrew bible, for instance, demands that punishment should fit the crime: 'an eye for an eye, a tooth for a tooth' – or in this case, a death for a death.

Opponents may point out that the logic of the *lex talionis* leads to unpalatable conclusions, such as that rapists should be raped, sadistic torturers tortured, and so on. And religious support is of course sought on the other side of the argument. Most religions teach that killing is wrong. The same Hebrew bible has many prohibitions against killing, including the divine commandment 'Thou shalt not kill.' Against this, those in favour of capital punishment maintain that the right to life is conditional. It is not considered wrong to take another's life in self-defence; in the same way, those who deliberately take the life of another forfeit their own right to life and can have no complaint when the state demands their life in return.

> **DOES CAPITAL PUNISHMENT TEND TO THE SECURITY OF THE PEOPLE? BY NO MEANS. IT HARDENS THE HEARTS OF MEN, AND MAKES THE LOSS OF LIFE APPEAR LIGHT TO THEM.**
>
> Elizabeth Fry, 1818

In the end, attempts to argue that judicial killing is essentially just or unjust are unlikely to succeed against entrenched views. One side sees capital punishment as an expression of society's righteous outrage at the most blatant infringement of its rules; the other sees it as an act of barbarism, a sort of revenge killing that debases society and brings it down to the level of the criminal. In such an impasse, debate is likely to turn to consideration of the consequences of the judicial use of the death penalty.

THE DEATH OF INNOCENTS

No murderer has been executed and reoffended; many murderers have been released or escaped from custody and murdered again. Therefore the use of capital punishment has saved innocent lives. This claim, which is

2011

Capital punishment is retained in 58 countries, the most active being China, Iran, Saudi Arabia, Iraq and the USA

2012

An estimated 20,000 people worldwide are living under sentence of death unquestionably true, is best countered by another no less certain: that the use of capital punishment has cost innocent lives. In every age, in every jurisdiction, miscarriages of justice have led to innocent people being executed. The truth is that perfection has never been achieved either in courts of law or in the operation of prisoner-release schemes. Unless we decide to prioritize one kind of victim over another, these arguments tend to cancel each other out.

Better off dead

An intriguing twist in the debate over capital punishment is given by cases such as that of Ian Brady, the Moors murderer who has been languishing in prison since 1965. Given that Brady has repeatedly expressed his wish to die, would it not be more humane to allow him to do so? The argument is then turned entirely on its head, for those who favour the death penalty as the sternest form of retribution, believing that the heaviest possible punishment should be visited on those guilty of the most heinous crimes, would presumably argue that Brady and his like should be kept alive in order to prolong their suffering.

PROTECTING OR DEBASING SOCIETY

Another claim used to justify capital punishment is that it protects the public by deterring would-be offenders. Opponents claim that the deterrent effect is at best unproven, but common sense suggests that the prospect of punishment by death must have *some* influence. Imagine a world in which all murderers were struck down, instantly, by a thunderbolt the moment they committed their crime. To suppose that people – rational people, at least – with murderous intentions, knowing that instant annihilation awaited them, would press ahead regardless is surely implausible. The problem is that, in the real world, the death penalty is usually neither certain nor swift: how much deterrent effect remains after years of judicial reviews and appeals is debatable.

This same fact puts paid to another, economic argument for the death penalty – the frequent complaint that we waste millions of pounds keeping killers in prison, often for decades. The reality is that years spent on Death Row, punctuated by numerous judicial appeals, are anything but a cheap alternative. Another point made against capital punishment is the demonstrable fact that it discriminates against the most impoverished and vulnerable members of society. Unless the state is prepared to fund better social provision for these disadvantaged members (including, but not limited to, improved legal representation), there is bound to be a basic unfairness in the application of the death penalty.

Opponents of capital punishment argue that, far from reducing the incidence of murder, it may actually increase it. For one thing, the state's sanctioning of the death penalty may lead to a cheapening of life, to a weakening of the taboo against killing: where society deems it appropriate to take life, is it not likely that respect for life will be widely eroded? Also, in jurisdictions where the death penalty is extended to serious offences other than murder, there is a phenomenon of crime escalation: if a rapist, say, knows that his victim's testimony is likely to cause his death, there appears to be a gruesome logic in his killing his victim.

A THORNY ISSUE

Debate over the death penalty is beset with contradictions. The deterrent effect, arguably its chief justification, demands a kind of swift and summary justice that would almost inevitably lead to an increase in the number of miscarriages and hence wrongful executions. The greater effectiveness of such a system would also, almost certainly, be gained at the cost of greater discrimination against the poor and disadvantaged. With so much uncertainty surrounding its claimed benefits, the argument tends to revert to the basic question of whether it is, in absolute terms, right for the state to take the lives of its members. And as we have seen, the issues there are no less thorny.

The best bet?

The best bet argument, first popularized by the Dutch-American sociologist Ernest van den Haag, starts from the premise that the deterrent value of capital punishment is unproven one way or the other. If the death penalty does in fact deter, its use will save innocent lives; if it does not, we will pointlessly execute murderers. Given the choice between saving victims and killing murderers, van den Haag has no doubt where we should put our money. The problem with his argument is that capital punishment may deter would-be murderers and yet still cost innocent lives – as a result of miscarriages of justice, for instance, and by eroding the social taboo against killing. Is the net saving of innocent life the measure by which we should judge the death penalty?

The condensed idea
Society's righteous outrage or revenge killing?

33 Torture

A terrorist group has planted a nuclear bomb in London, timed to go off in two hours. There is not enough time to launch an evacuation of the area, so it is inevitable that if the bomb goes off, many thousands of innocent people will die. The police, who know about the device but not its location, have captured the leader of the terrorist group, who knows where it is but refuses to talk. Is it right for the police to use torture in an attempt to force the terrorist to cooperate?

The kneejerk reaction to torture, at least among those raised in free democracies, is that it is completely unacceptable and has no place in a civilized society subject to the rule of law. But cases like the ticking-bomb scenario sketched out above test such intuitions to breaking-point. If the threat is imminent and no other course of action is available, is it not morally acceptable – indeed, morally obligatory – to do whatever can be done to avert the catastrophe? The captured terrorist is himself responsible for the crisis, so to infringe his rights, by subjecting him to torture, seems a small price to pay to save the lives of thousands.

In recent years, and especially since the 9/11 terrorist attacks, there has been a new urgency about issues such as torture and its use to obtain intelligence considered vital in fighting the 'war against terrorism'. A host of strange terms, from 'waterboarding' to 'extraordinary rendition', have entered the lexicon of political debate. So is it ever morally justified to use torture?

TIMELINE

1984	September 11, 2001
The UN Convention against Torture requires states to prevent the use of torture within their borders	The 9/11 attacks provoke debate over the balance between national security and human rights

The problem of dirty hands

Some hard-line commentators – unusually candid – claim that it is naïve to suppose that politicians could ever keep their hands entirely clean: to serve the public's interests, they inevitably, on occasion, have to violate fundamental moral principles. Torturers themselves, however, are usually less frank about the nature of their calling, and governments all over the world habitually twist their words to cover their trail. For this reason, in the case of torture, matters of definition really matter. In 2004 a leaked CIA report suggested that the US government had approved interrogation techniques that violated the 1984 United Nations Convention

against Torture, according to which torture is the 'cruel, inhumane or degrading' infliction of severe pain or suffering, mental or physical, in order to obtain information. The White House was accused by critics of redefining torture as techniques that result in severe harm to a bodily organ, thereby allowing its agents to use methods such as sleep deprivation and waterboarding, in which a detainee is forced underwater and suffers the sensation of drowning. The issue of 'dirty hands', which questions the extent to which governments can attend to the security of their people without resorting to immoral practices such as torture, has never been more alive.

NASTY ENDS AND NASTY MEANS

Faced with the kind of extreme scenario presented above, most people concede, reluctantly, that it is morally right for torture to be used – provided that there really are no other alternatives. The grounds for this view are essentially consequentialist. There are two, and only two, courses that the police can follow, both of which are highly unpalatable. They can use torture to extract information from the guilty terrorist, whose human rights will thereby be temporarily violated. Or they can allow the incineration of thousands of innocent people, whose right to life will thereby be permanently violated.

Choosing the first option – to use torture – can be opposed on absolutist grounds. Some insist that torture is wrong in principle and should not be used under any circumstances. If absolutists are prepared to stomach the

2001–10

The TV series *24* portrays extensive and effective use of torture

2002

Controversy surrounds interrogation techniques used at the US detention centre at Guantanamo Bay in Cuba

consequences of the ticking-bomb scenario, it is hard to see how they can be shifted from their ground. A more generally persuasive case against torture, however, can be made by answering the consequentialist in kind. Simply doing the maths in these extreme scenarios, an opponent may argue, might indicate that torture is justified, but many broader considerations have been left out of the equation.

TOWARDS A TORTURE CULTURE

One familiar objection to torture is simply that it is ineffective. People subjected to extreme pain or suffering are inclined to say anything to make it go away; they are likely to say whatever they think their interrogators wish to hear, so the quality of the intelligence is poor.

A more subtle argument against torture is based on its supposed impact on a society in which it is used. Where torture techniques are routinely practised, a 'torture culture' may develop, which is barbaric in itself and debases society. Institutions such as the military, police, security and prison services easily fall into habits of mistreating individuals, and torture would become all-pervasive if such treatment were both accepted and legal. In short, accepting the use of torture in extreme cases rapidly leads to a culture in which it becomes routine and institutionalized; the damage done to the fabric of society is so deep that it cannot be justified by its (supposedly) good consequences in exceptional, one-off emergencies.

STOPPING THE SLIDE

This argument against torture assumes that there is a slippery slope that leads inexorably from the extraordinary use of torture to routine, legalized and institutionalized use. But is such a descent inevitable? For one thing, it does not follow that an act that is morally permissible in some highly specific and exceptional circumstances should be legalized. The law is typically based on generalized rules that are derived by a process of abstraction from particular cases; cases such as the ticking-bomb scenario are, by definition, exceptional, one-off events that are unprecedented and themselves set no precedent. We might accept, again reluctantly, that it is morally permissible for the survivors of a plane crash to stay alive by eating the flesh of their dead fellow passengers, but there is no suggestion that such exceptional events provide a reason to legalize cannibalism.

Jack Bauer, tortured hero of torture

According to its critics, nothing has done more to normalize the use of torture in the minds of ordinary Americans than the popular TV series *24*. Some ingenious variant of the ticking-bomb scenario is central to each of *24*'s eight seasons, and in each case torture is represented as both necessary and effective in combating the terrorist threat. Torture is institutionalized within the fictional Counter-Terrorism Unit (CTU) – there are special agents whose sole function is to torture suspects – while *24*'s hero (or perhaps 'hero'), Jack Bauer, frequently resorts to torture to extract (invariably, with success) intelligence vital to the security of the United States. Those who place obstacles in Bauer's way – complacent liberals, spineless politicians and naïve human-rights advocates – are consistently portrayed as misguided and contemptible. Nevertheless, the picture is not entirely one-sided, as Bauer himself – both user and victim of torture – becomes more and more physically haggard and psychologically scarred as the series progresses. There can be little doubt that *24*, however partisan in its own take on the matter, has played a significant role in shaping the popular debate on torture.

Much the same can be said of the one-off use of torture. Torture is morally abhorrent, and there are very strong grounds for saying that its practice should remain illegal. Those who commit acts of torture should be prosecuted, albeit that very considerable mitigation should be allowed in the quite exceptional circumstances surrounding cases similar to the ticking-bomb scenario. Although the slippery slope imagined by opponents is perhaps not inevitable, much has happened in recent years – the US army detention centres in Abu Ghraib in Iraq and Guantanamo Bay in Cuba are only the best-publicized instances – to suggest that the utmost vigilance is needed if torture and other extra-judicial practices are not to spread their corrosive effects more widely through society.

The condensed idea
A necessary evil?

34 Corruption

Corruption is a process by which the virtue or integrity of someone or something is progressively undermined or destroyed. It is one thing for a good and upright person to be led astray, quite another for a sound and efficient institution to go bad. Nevertheless, although institutional and personal corruption are clearly distinct, they have much in common and often occur together.

Virtuous people are those disposed to do what is right, however that is defined – much of this book is an attempt to address precisely that issue. Views differ on the detail of how such people should behave, but they may variously be honest, just, generous, courageous, tolerant, forgiving, respectful, temperate and hard-working, among other things. The precise set of conditions that have to be met for us to say that such people have been corrupted might be quite complex, but there must at least be some kind of inducement that causes them to stop behaving in one or more of these virtuous ways. The inducement might be financial gain – they might be bribed to behave dishonestly, for example – but there are many other possible motivations: the promise of enhanced status or power, for instance, or sexual favours.

FROM PERSONAL TO INSTITUTIONAL CORRUPTION

Other examples of personal corruption include cases where a witness gives false testimony in court in order to prevent a friend being convicted, perhaps in the belief that the friend is innocent; or where a police officer fabricates evidence in order to secure a conviction, perhaps in the belief that the suspect

TIMELINE

1993	1999
Transparency International is founded to raise awareness of corruption	The OECD Anti-Bribery Convention comes into force

is guilty. These instances of personal corruption show how they are often linked to institutional corruption. The purpose of the judicial system, one of the state's central institutions, is to administer justice, and there are various processes, such as the giving of truthful testimony and the presentation of genuine evidence, that enable the system to achieve its purpose. The actions of the false witness and the dishonest police officer undermine the essential processes of the judicial system and thereby help to subvert its main purpose; the institution is therefore compromised and corrupted to some degree.

> **AMONG A PEOPLE GENERALLY CORRUPT, LIBERTY CANNOT LONG EXIST.**
>
> Edmund Burke,
> Irish political theorist, 1777

Extrapolating from these cases, we may say that any institution has a purpose for which it was established, and various processes by which it realizes this

In search of transparency

Attempts at tackling corruption worldwide have been held back by a lack of basic data. The scale of the problem is hard to gauge accurately, as corrupt dealings are by their nature clandestine, while any kind of comparative analysis is hampered by the fact that such data as there is comes from a wide range of different places and different contexts. One of the leading non-governmental organizations active in combating corruption, Transparency International, has attempted to improve the objectivity of its data by adopting a neutral definition of corruption as 'abuse of entrusted power for private gain'. The underlying assumption here is that power is granted to officials, by the people or otherwise, on condition that it is used for the benefit of society as a whole, so to use it for personal gain is an illegal breach of trust. Corruption, on this view, is interpreted merely as an illegal exchange – a preferential grant of a benefit from an official to a recipient, in return for some sort of bribe (monetary or other). Today, Transparency International publishes a number of surveys and reports, the best known of which is the Corruption Perceptions Index, which measures perceived levels of public-sector corruption in 183 countries and territories around the world.

2006

Barack Obama addresses the issue of corruption on a visit to Kenya

The finger of blame

Corruption may be especially rife in developing countries, but the West must bear a large share of the responsibility for this ugly state of affairs. Many of the bribes – and almost all the biggest bribes – are offered by Western companies and giant multinationals seeking to win major leases, concessions and contracts. Indeed, it was not until 1999 that any effort was made to introduce sanctions against bribery in international business transactions, when the Organization for Economic Cooperation and Development (OECD) established a convention that required signatories to criminalize the act of bribing foreign public officials. Arguably this has done less to eradicate bribery than to provide employment for company lawyers seeking ways of circumventing the rules.

purpose. Such an institution is corrupted, to some degree, by actions that undermine its processes and thereby prevent it from achieving its purpose. As in the case of personal corruption, financial gain may be the motivation, but other inducements, such as the promise of enhanced status or power, may be involved as well or instead.

Every institution has rules and regulations, more or less explicit, and the observance of these is intended to make its processes work efficiently and thereby to realize its purpose. Any corrupt act must necessarily break these rules and so be 'illegal' within the institution's own jurisdiction. Coaches who give performance-enhancing drugs to their athletes may break the rules laid down by the relevant sport's governing body; their cheating has a corrupting effect on the particular sport as an institution, as well as on sport more generally and on various 'sub-institutions' or cultures implicit within sport, such as the institution of fair play. Whether or not such an act is illegal in the broader sense of breaking the state's laws is another matter.

A GLOBAL CANCER
It is vital to understand what corruption is and why it occurs, because it is without question one of the major scourges in the world today. The corrosive effects of financial corruption on every aspect of a country's existence was

the focus of a speech by Senator Barack Obama, soon-to-be 44th president of the United States, on a visit to Kenya in 2006:

> Corruption stifles development – it siphons off scarce resources that could improve infrastructure, bolster education systems, and strengthen public health ... In the end, if the people cannot trust their government to do the job for which it exists – to protect them and to promote their common welfare – all else is lost.

While no country is immune to corruption, its impact is most acutely felt in developing countries, where political institutions are typically more vulnerable and official procedures and safeguards less robust. In such circumstances, it is relatively easy for a culture of fraud, bribery and extortion to take root. As public funds and resources are diverted into private pockets, poverty spreads among the general population, generating cynicism about political processes as it does so. Where political leaders are seen to be unaccountable and 'on the make', it is almost impossible for democratic institutions and respect for the rule of law to take

CORRUPTION ... ERODES THE STATE FROM THE INSIDE OUT, SICKENING THE JUSTICE SYSTEM UNTIL THERE IS NO JUSTICE TO BE FOUND, POISONING THE POLICE FORCES UNTIL THEIR PRESENCE BECOMES A SOURCE OF INSECURITY RATHER THAN COMFORT.
Barack Obama, 2006

root. For these reasons corruption is one of the main causes of the world's most pressing problems – weak governance, growing poverty, poor health and healthcare, inadequate education – and tackling it is one of mankind's greatest challenges.

The condensed idea
A cancer at the heart of the state

35 Terrorism

'One man's terrorist is another man's freedom fighter.' It may be something of a cliché, but there is an important grain of truth in this saying. Today, the word 'terrorism' always has a strongly negative meaning: nobody uses the word to describe themselves. A state tends to see any violence directed against itself, except violence from another state, as terroristic, while it portrays its own actions as legitimate acts of war or defence against its enemies. These enemies, on the other hand, see themselves as warriors, sometimes even martyrs, fighting in a just cause.

When the term is loaded in this way, debate over the ethics of terrorism is fruitless. A terrorist action is wrong by definition, merely by virtue of being described as such. This is not to say that it is a purely semantic issue and therefore doesn't matter: sometimes it is vital to win the war of words – to win over the 'hearts and minds' of participants and observers alike. Yet we need to get beyond the semantic impasse if we are to say anything interesting, ethically, about the concept of terrorism.

VIOLENCE AND INTIMIDATION

The state calls a given act an illicit act of terrorism; the perpetrators of the act call it a legitimate act of political violence. The state's understanding of itself implicit here is in accord with the influential view of the German sociologist Max Weber, who suggested that the defining characteristic of the state was its claimed 'monopoly on the legitimate use of physical force': the exclusive right, in other words, to make laws within its territory and to use violence,

TIMELINE

1890s–1900s	1922
Revolutionary anarchists target political leaders including French president Marie-François Sadi Carnot (1894) and US president William McKinley (1901)	Max Weber's *Economy and Society*, published posthumously, analyses the relationship between violence and the state

actual or threatened, to force compliance with those laws. The perpetrators of violence against a particular state might, indeed, accept this definition; they contend, however, that the state which they oppose has, for some reason, forfeited its rights as a state and is therefore a legitimate target of violence.

On both sides, then, there is agreement that terrorism involves violence. And there is more common ground: this violence is carried out with the specific intention of creating terror – using intimidation to achieve some further political goal. Broadly, the two parties agree on what is done (violence) and why it is done (to intimidate). The chief point of difference is the legitimacy of the goal, and it is this that determines whether a particular act of violence is labelled as terrorism or political violence.

TARGETING THE INNOCENT

Acts commonly called acts of terrorism can take many different forms. Consider the following two scenarios:

1 *Clandestine organization A, fighting for liberation from a colonial power, plants a bomb in the governor's residence; it explodes and kills the governor and a number of government officials.*

2 *Clandestine organization B, also fighting for liberation, plants a bomb in a popular tourist hotel, killing a random selection of foreign visitors, indigenous hotel workers and others.*

Would we describe both of these scenarios as terrorist attacks? Perhaps, but they clearly have a very different complexion. Targeting members of the government, as in the first scenario, might have some intimidatory value, but it could perhaps be better described as a focused attempt to weaken the government by eliminating key personnel. The colonial power would doubtless

2001

The 9/11 Islamist attacks on the USA mark the climax of 'new' terrorism

2003

The USA and the 'coalition of the willing' invade Iraq

present the attack as terroristic, but the perpetrators themselves would regard their victims as legitimate targets – as official representatives of what they see as an illegitimate regime – and would probably describe their operation as an assassination rather than an act of terrorism.

In the second scenario the situation is very different. Crucially, the victims are selected or targeted only in the vaguest sense: an impartial view would be that they are innocent bystanders or non-combatants, with no (clear or direct) responsibility for the grievances that motivate the bombers. And the objective of the attack is very diffuse. The aims probably include demonstrating the organization's power to inflict harm and the government's inability to prevent it; undermining the country's economy by deterring tourists, foreign investors, etc.; intimidating and destabilizing, in a completely unfocused manner, the ruling regime. Nobody, except presumably the perpetrators themselves, would describe the operation as anything other than an act of terrorism.

IS TERRORISM EVER JUSTIFIED?

From an ethical standpoint, it makes a great deal of difference if both the scenarios sketched out above are seen as terrorist attacks, or just the second. It is commonly claimed by the perpetrators of such attacks that their victims are in some way complicit in causing the grievances that provide the broad justification for their actions. Such a claim is highly plausible in the first scenario, the bombing of the governor's residence, but much less so in the second, the attack on the hotel. Following the 9/11 attacks on the United States, the al-Qaeda leader Osama bin Laden claimed that all Americans were responsible for atrocities committed against Muslims, on the grounds that they were collectively responsible for electing the government, paying taxes, etc. The idea that paying money (often grudgingly) to the Internal Revenue Service is sufficient grounds for being incinerated in aviation fuel is grotesque in itself – to say nothing of the many people (including babies) who do not vote or pay taxes.

Complicity, then, looks like a plausible justification for attacks that target those who are genuinely complicit – though there are doubts whether such attacks are best described as terroristic. But it takes a very far-fetched view of collective responsibility for complicity to justify the kind of random attacks

Sacrifice on the altar of extremism

Terrorists tend to be driven by extreme views, perhaps because it is only such people who can contemplate 'sacrificing' innocent lives in pursuit of a greater goal. At the turn of the 20th century an extreme doctrine known as revolutionary anarchism spread bloody mayhem across Europe and North America. Its adherents held that the impact of the state on its citizens was so dire that it warranted forcible removal by any means, including violence. The underlying idea was that new life emerged from annihilation, or, as the Russian anarchist Mikhail Bakunin portentously put it, 'the urge for destruction is also a creative urge'. The upshot was a spate of terrorist attacks on high-profile leaders and politicians, including kings, presidents and prime ministers, whose assassinations were intended to highlight the vulnerability of the state and so inspire the masses to revolution. At the turn of the 21st century, the 9/11 attacks on the United States were the worst (though not the first) manifestations of a new brand of terrorism marked by religious fanaticism. Accountable only to God, these 'new' terrorists, most notably the Islamist group al-Qaeda, were quite willing to sacrifice their own lives in order to maximize the deaths of their enemies, including non-combatants. As such they remained (and remain) incomprehensible to their enemies, presenting a threat that has not yet been fully understood, let alone adequately countered.

that generally result in the death and maiming of those who would normally be considered innocent non-combatants. Are there any better justifications?

An ethical consequentialist – one who judges the rightness and wrongness of actions purely on the basis of their consequences – would regard a terrorist attack on non-combatants as justified if it resulted in a sufficiently large benefit, all things considered. This qualification is important, for among the things considered should be whether this benefit could be achieved in a less morally repugnant manner (for instance, by targeting those who *are* complicit in some way). Many would say that there must *always* be a better way than taking the lives of innocents, and that weighing up the pros and cons, in the consequentialist manner, is not the right way to reach a verdict in such cases. Thus the issue of terrorism resolves itself, once again, into the intractable conflict in ethics between ends and means.

The condensed idea
The power of intimidation

36 Censorship

Freedom of speech and expression is so highly prized in the Western world that it is sometimes unthinkingly supposed that censorship is necessarily bad. Such a view is naïve, and in reality there have always been significant checks on free speech. In every age, to differing degrees, society's leaders have assumed the right to control the behaviour of their subjects or citizens, by regulating the flow of information and blocking the expression of opinions they considered dangerous.

The liberal commitment to freedom of expression has its origins in the 17th-century Enlightenment and is most notably underwritten by the First Amendment (1791) to the US Constitution, which includes the provision that 'Congress shall make no law … abridging the freedom of speech, or of the press.' In practice, though, even in the most liberal regimes, there is a range of laws to punish those who abuse this freedom by expressing views or disclosing information in ways that the state regards as unacceptable: laws protecting official secrets and criminalizing libel, obscenity, blasphemy and various kinds of incitement are all forms of censorship. The big ethical question, then, is not whether there should be censorship – very few suggest that completely unfettered free speech is practicable or desirable. The issue is to decide how and where to draw the lines.

WHEN THE STATE KNOWS BEST
The prevailing view before the Enlightenment – near-universal until that time and still common now – was essentially authoritarian, or at best paternalistic.

TIMELINE

1644	1791
John Milton's *Areopagitica* argues against the licensing of books	The First Amendment of the US Constitution guarantees freedom of speech and of the press

The porn wars

If pornography is a key battleground in the debate over censorship, it is a field deeply enveloped in the fog of war. Historically, the debate has seen moral conservatives on one side, convinced that sexually explicit material is socially damaging because it threatens traditional (including family and religious) values; and liberals on the other, insisting that it is ultimately a matter of private choice and that consenting adults should be allowed to produce and consume such material, provided that their doing so does not harm others. Unfortunately, proof of harm – does production of pornography involve the coercion or exploitation of actors? does consumption increase sexual violence? – has to date been inconclusive. In recent decades the debate has been revitalized by feminists, who argue that pornography – violent and/or degrading pornography, at least – endorses female subordination (by treating women as sex objects, for instance) and thereby institutionalizes male superiority and infringes women's right to equal civil status. Pornography, according to this view, is an issue of human rights – something that the liberal cannot easily ignore.

Societies were typically arranged in strict hierarchies in which a governing elite would exercise extensive powers of censorship over the governed, presuming to determine what kinds of expression were permitted in many aspects of life. Authoritarian regimes generally controlled the flow of information in their own interest, suppressing views that they regarded as a threat to their survival.

Authoritarian use of censorship can show a more benign face, however. A governing class or elite may decide what forms of expression are permitted on a paternalistic basis: in effect, the state assumes that it knows best, but not what is best for *itself* (or itself alone) but what is best for its *members*. How does the state know this? The answer is usually a combination of religious and

1859

John Stuart Mill's *On Liberty* argues that only harm to others justifies limiting free speech

1891

Oscar Wilde's *The Soul of Man under Socialism* is published

Art and the censor

One of the trickiest aspects of censorship is to draw a credible line between ethics and aesthetics. 'There is no such thing as a moral book or an immoral book,' wrote Oscar Wilde in 1891. 'Books are well written or badly written. That is all.' A perennial concern is that the dead hand of the censor makes dull art. Picasso insisted that true art could not thrive in the sterile atmosphere created by the censor: 'Art is never chaste. It ought to be forbidden to ignorant innocents, never allowed into contact with those not sufficiently prepared. Yes, art is dangerous. Where it is chaste, it is not art.' George Bernard Shaw made the same point for literary art, observing that censorship reaches its logical conclusion 'when nobody is allowed to read any books except the books nobody reads'. And John Milton, in his *Areopagitica* of 1644 – perhaps the most famous of all literary attacks on censorship – argues that the goodness of good books is only fully apparent to a reader who can judge them alongside bad ones. Truth, he protests, will always prevail over falsehood 'in a free and open encounter'; if evil is banished, it is impossible to 'praise a fugitive and cloistered virtue'.

cultural influences. The state's aim, essentially conservative in character, is to protect a body of values – often including rather fuzzy 'family' values – that may be based on religious teaching and passed down from generation to generation. Those in power have a clear view of what is morally right and wrong, or so they think, and decide on that basis what is acceptable in order to promote the moral well-being of ordinary people. In effect, the state takes on the duty of shaping the moral character of its members, and to this end assumes the right to limit expression of, or exposure to, things that are likely to 'deprave and corrupt' that character.

HARM, OFFENCE AND SOCIETY'S FROWN

One of the core values of liberalism is autonomy – the idea that people should be in control of their destiny, free to make decisions on their own account and without interference from others. Accordingly, liberals are generally opposed to all forms of paternalism, however well-intentioned they may be. According to the classic account given by the Victorian philosopher John Stuart Mill, freedom of expression should be restricted only if not doing so would cause harm to others (*see chapter 10*). In essence, people should be at liberty to do – and think and say and otherwise express themselves – as they please, provided that their doing so is consistent with others doing likewise. They may legitimately be advised and educated about any harm they risk doing to themselves by their chosen behaviour, but this is not ultimately a sufficient reason to curtail their freedom to behave in that way.

The devil, of course, is in the detail. Some people are much more susceptible to harm than others. And with the growth of the internet and social media, a vast array of new ways of harming people and their interests has opened up. To suggest that a leading public figure is a paedophile may clearly do harm to his reputation. But what of a footballer who collapses on the field, then becomes the target of tasteless jokes on Twitter or other social networks? Is sufficient harm done to him – or perhaps to society in general – to warrant some kind of legal action? The issue here is drawing a line between (actual) harm and (mere) offence. But, again, offence is a highly subjective matter, and in some such cases fear of social disapproval may be a more effective deterrent than the law's heavy hand.

> **WHENEVER BOOKS ARE BURNED, IN THE END MEN TOO ARE BURNED.**
> Heinrich Heine,
> German poet, 1821

Mill himself was aware of the role played by social censure in curtailing liberty of expression. Indeed, he was concerned that such pressure could sometimes exercise a stifling and unhealthy control, promoting a culture of intellectual repression, in which questioning and criticism of received opinion is discouraged and 'the most active and inquiring intellects' are afraid to enter into 'free and daring speculation on the highest subjects'. The upshot, he believes, is that mental development becomes cramped, reason cowed, and truth itself weakly rooted: 'true opinion abides ... as a prejudice, a belief independent of, and proof against, argument ... Truth, thus held, is but one superstition the more, accidentally clinging to the words which enunciate a truth.'

The condensed idea
The morality of the muzzle

37 Drugs

The extent of human misery associated with the use and abuse of illegal drugs is not seriously in doubt. Addicts often live short and squalid lives, thieving and prostituting themselves to feed their habit, catching and spreading diseases by sharing dirty needles, blighting the lives of their families and children. Many more are caught up in the illegal trafficking of drugs, a global industry in which producer countries in the developing world are beggared by billionaire gangsters and business rivals are routinely murdered.

What is less clear is precisely where to lay the blame for this litany of misery. For it can be argued that many of the drug-related problems that are blighting millions of lives are not due so much to the use of drugs as to the attempts of governments to prohibit their use. The issue of legalization defines much of the debate over drug use, and for the most part this debate is conducted in the heat of party politics, not in the spirit of honest inquiry. Intensely politicized, the central questions are usually treated inconsistently, disingenuously, even hypocritically.

Yet the answers matter. Tens of billions of dollars are spent each year in attempts to eradicate the production and distribution of drugs such as cannabis, cocaine and heroin. Hundreds of thousands of people are locked up in prisons on the assumption that drug use is wrong. Can we cut through the fog of disinformation and say whether that assumption is correct?

TIMELINE

1839–42, 1856–60	1961	1988
Two Opium Wars are fought between Britain and China	The Single Convention on Narcotic Drugs is signed in New York	The UN Convention against Illicit Traffic in Narcotic Drugs is signed at Vienna

ARE ALL DRUGS THE SAME?

The case for prohibiting the use of drugs is based on various kinds of harm that they are believed to cause – to users themselves, to those around them and to society in general. Prohibition is often associated with a conservative perspective, but even liberals accept that governments should try to stop people behaving in ways that cause (certain kinds of) harm to others (*see chapter 10*). Few would propose that people under the influence of drugs should be allowed to drive cars or operate fork-lift trucks, for instance. Beyond this, though, there is little common ground.

One problem that constantly besets the issue of drugs is a tendency, in political debate if not in law, to lump all drugs together. The reality is that some drugs are much more harmful than others. There are lots of things that cause as much harm as 'soft' drugs, such as cannabis, and yet are not subject to criminal sanctions. Alcohol is more addictive than cannabis, according to some experts, and statistically it is more likely to kill you, damage your health, ruin your personal relationships and undermine your financial situation. Much the same can be said of tobacco, but few would suggest that drinkers and smokers should be branded as criminals for their habits. Hard drugs, on the other hand, such as heroin and crack cocaine, are usually much more harmful; they are highly addictive, often producing an obsessive dependence that causes much harm

The long view

The current intensity of concern over the illegal use of drugs is relatively recent. In the middle of the 19th century, Britain fought two wars with China in order to *uphold* its right to trade in opium. It was only in the following century that the first efforts were made to eradicate the international drugs trade – efforts that culminated in the Single Convention on Narcotic Drugs (1961) and various United Nations-sponsored initiatives to prohibit drug production and supply. Over the centuries most societies have taken a more relaxed view. Alcohol is the accepted drug of choice in the West today, but a wide range of substances found to have mind- or mood-altering properties have been no less acceptable at other times and in other places.

1998

Mark McGwire breaks the single-season home run record

1999–2005

Lance Armstrong wins seven consecutive Tours de France

A tainted legacy: drugs in sport

In 1998 baseball slugger Mark McGwire hit 70 home runs, an astonishing nine more than the record set 37 years earlier; the following year US cyclist Lance Armstrong won the first of a record seven consecutive Tour de France victories. At the time these feats were ranked among the greatest in any sport; now they are tainted by the revelation that the record-breakers were fuelled by performance-enhancing drugs (PEDs). The essence of sport is fair competition: the playing field must be level and the game played in the right spirit. So the use of steroids and other substances banned by a game's governing body is an utter subversion of everything that sport represents, sacrificing the public trust that is its life-blood. As the sports writer Tom Verducci said of baseball's infamous 'Steroid Era', 'Trust in a fair game was being depleted as jobs and games were being decided by who had the best chemist.'

both to users and to others connected to them. The kind of inconsistency seen in drug policy causes widespread scepticism, not least among the many millions who make occasional use of soft drugs, apparently without any seriously adverse effects.

There is certainly a much stronger case for legal prohibition of hard drugs. Many liberals insist, nevertheless, that any legal restriction on drug use is wrong, arguing that we have a fundamental right to do as we wish with our own bodies and that the various harms caused by drug use are not of the kind that governments should seek to control. To moral conservatives, such permissiveness seems complacent and irresponsible. Some drugs are considered so addictive that they effectively limit the user's ability to act freely and hence undermine their personal autonomy. Liberalism may require that people are given sufficient liberal rope to hang themselves. Still – given that autonomy is, for liberals, the ethical capacity *par excellence* – there is some tension in their position if they insist that people should have freedom even at the cost of their character as moral agents.

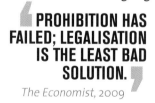

PROHIBITION HAS FAILED; LEGALISATION IS THE LEAST BAD SOLUTION.

The Economist, 2009

APRÈS CELA, LE DÉLUGE?

In the end, the drugs issue tends to take a pragmatic turn. Legalizers point to the ineffectiveness of current policies, arguing that governments stand Canute-like against the relentlessly rising tide of use and that their stance is increasingly out of step with popular sentiment and practice. Prohibitionists, on the other hand, typically paint a picture of catastrophic and epidemic abuse in the wake of legalization. So what would really happen if drugs were decriminalized?

The available evidence, such as it is, does not suggest that catastrophe would ensue. The most important consequence would be that drug abuse could be treated not as a criminal activity but as a healthcare issue. The drug trade, taken out of the hands of criminals, could be regulated and the quality of its products properly monitored; prices would fall and taxes could be gathered. Resources, financial and other, currently dedicated to policing and incarceration, could be channelled into research, rehabilitation and education, which – the evidence of tobacco suggests – would lead in time to more moderate usage. Most important of all, perhaps, more attention could be given to the social deprivation and lack of opportunity that drive some of the most desperate people to resort to drugs in the first place.

The implications of decriminalization are, to some degree, a matter of speculation – and many would say that the analysis given by the legalization lobby is dangerously naïve. Speculation should, at any rate, be well informed, and the minimum requirement for that is open and honest debate. The prospects of any such candour, in the current political climate, are bleak.

The condensed idea
Controlling the trade in misery – and pleasure

38 Animal liberation

In the past half-century the issue of animal welfare has moved from the margins of public debate to take a central place. The space of a few decades has witnessed the emergence of a major political movement that has attracted millions of supporters worldwide. This explosion of activism was originally sparked by the work of a few academic philosophers, who in the 1970s started to voice concerns over the abuse and exploitation of non-human animals, primarily in research and food production.

A seminal event in the struggle for animal liberation, or animal rights, came in 1975 with the publication of the Australian philosopher Peter Singer's book *Animal Liberation*. After analysing the appalling conditions commonly found in factory farms and research laboratories, Singer questions the low moral status accorded to animals and argues that their interests need to be considered alongside those of humans.

Is it right, then, that thousands of monkeys and apes, not to mention millions of rats, mice, cats and dogs, are used in medical research and product-testing? Is it right that literally billions of animals such as cows, sheep, pigs and chickens are slaughtered to provide us with meat?

'THINGS' UNDER MAN'S DOMINION

The name of the modern movement emphasized the feeling that animals needed liberation, not (merely) humane treatment. There were echoes of the movement for women's liberation, which sought equal rights for women

TIMELINE

4th century BC	4th–5th century AD	17th century
Aristotle places human beings at the top of his hierarchy of life	St Augustine asserts that animals exist only to serve mankind	René Descartes believes that animals are like automata, with no consciousness

Are rights right?

The animal liberation movement is often referred to as the animal *rights* movement, and the main bone of contention – the question of how much moral value (if any) we should attribute to animals – is often presented as a matter of rights. But is it helpful to introduce the notion of rights? The idea of rights is laden with conceptual baggage – they are supposed to impose duties on their bearers, or to entail claims that can be brought against others, or to involve some kind of reciprocity: exactly the kind of duties and relationships, in fact, that could never actually or literally exist between humans and animals. Many feel instinctively that animals, or at least some animals, deserve humane treatment – treatment that they often do not currently receive. How that common feeling is explained and theorized is important, but there is a danger that it becomes obscured or forgotten if the argument is resolved into a false dichotomy between having rights and not having rights.

and freedom from male dominance, but perhaps more significant was the implication that animals required release from bondage or servitude. Animals have generally been classified in law as 'legal things', signifying that they are merely objects to be owned, used and disposed of by 'legal persons' (i.e. humans). As such, animals have precisely the status of human slaves, enjoying no rights of their own and protected in law only as the legal property of their owners.

For the most part, until recent times, lawyers, philosophers and theologians have been broadly in agreement over the moral status of animals. The prevailing biblical view is that animals, lacking souls, were placed by God under man's dominion. St Augustine supports this view, insisting that animals exist only for the benefit of humans, while Thomas Aquinas suggests that the only reason to avoid treating them cruelly is the danger that such habits may carry over into our dealings with fellow humans.

1785

According to Immanuel Kant, animals are not rational and hence have no intrinsic moral value

1789

Jeremy Bentham argues that animals' suffering is the key issue in determining their moral worth

1975

Peter Singer's *Animal Liberation* inspires the modern animal liberation movement

1983

Tom Regan argues that animals merit rights as 'subjects of a life'

There have always been dissenting philosophical voices, but Aristotle in the fourth century BC set the prevailing tone with his view that there is a hierarchy of all living things in which the function of lower forms is to serve the needs of those higher in the 'chain of being' – which for Aristotle meant humans, by virtue of their rationality. Immanuel Kant, whose whole ethical theory is founded on the supremacy of reason, is in accord with this, believing that animals are not rational and hence have no moral value in themselves. Most hostile of all is Descartes, who regarded animals as little more than automata, whose movements were no proof of any inner feeling or intelligence.

OF CHIMPS AND CHICKENS

Chief among the dissenting voices was that of the English utilitarian philosopher Jeremy Bentham, who anticipated the animal liberation movement by nearly two centuries. With great prescience he wrote in 1789:

> The day may come when the rest of animal creation may acquire those rights which never could have been withholden from them but by the hand of tyranny ... a full-grown horse or dog is beyond comparison a more rational, as well as a more conversable animal, than an infant of a day, or a week, or even a month, old. But suppose they were otherwise, what would it avail? The question is not, Can they *reason?* nor Can they *talk?* but, *Can they suffer?*

In considering the moral status of animals, recent philosophers who take their lead from Bentham have moved beyond 'suffering', narrowly conceived. They propose that we should take into account not only the pain and pleasure experienced by animals but also such attributes as their intelligence and autonomy.

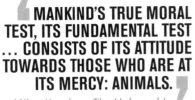

MANKIND'S TRUE MORAL TEST, ITS FUNDAMENTAL TEST ... CONSISTS OF ITS ATTITUDE TOWARDS THOSE WHO ARE AT ITS MERCY: ANIMALS.

Milan Kundera, *The Unbearable Lightness of Being*, 1984

For a utilitarian such as Singer, overall well-being, to which the experience of pleasure and pain contributes, is the measure of whether something is right or wrong; and he proposes that both human and non-human interests should be given equal consideration in such assessments. This does not mean that a chicken and a human should necessarily be treated the same, but the issue should not be decided in advance, purely on the basis of the fact that humans are humans. To show such preference, in the absence of any morally relevant difference between the cases, is an instance of 'speciesism' – a perspective akin to racism and sexism, which exhibit similar prejudice on the basis of race and sex (*see page 157*). So, if it is determined that a chicken kept in dire conditions in a battery suffers more than we do by being deprived of its meat, our consumption of the meat, and the farming methods used to produce it, are morally wrong.

A supporter of using (say) chimpanzees in medical research might argue, again on utilitarian grounds, that it is justified because the suffering caused to animals is outweighed by the benefits such research brings in the form of new drugs and technologies. But, if Singer's argument is right, these same benefits would justify using a brain-damaged human instead of a healthy chimpanzee, provided that the overall suffering caused to the human (and any others affected) was less than that endured by the chimpanzee.

This kind of conclusion is surprising, perhaps even shocking, but it follows as a matter of logical consistency – provided that we agree that a speciesist perspective is something that we should avoid. Even then, there remain formidable difficulties, both practical and theoretical (*see chapter 39*). For how on earth are we to determine the suffering of a battery chicken?

> ## Animals as subjects of a life
>
> Much of the intellectual bedrock underlying the modern animal liberation movement has been laid down by the utilitarian philosopher Peter Singer. The argument does not depend on a utilitarian perspective, however. Another influential voice in the movement is the US philosopher Tom Regan, who argues that animals – animals above a certain level of complexity, at least – should enjoy basic moral rights because they possess cognitive abilities similar to those that justify conferring such rights on humans. Such animals are 'subjects of a life', in Regan's words, and inherently valuable. As such, their rights are violated when they are treated instrumentally, as a means to an end – as a source of meat, for instance, or as subjects of experimentation or product-testing.

The condensed idea
Animal rights, animal wrongs

The research paradox

'The cruel experimenter cannot be allowed to have it both ways. He cannot, in the same breath, defend the scientific validity of vivisection on the grounds of the physical similarities between man and the other animals, and then defend the morality of vivisection on the grounds that men and animals are physically different. The only logical alternatives for him are to admit he is either pre-Darwinian or immoral.'

Writing in 1971, Richard Ryder, one of the pioneers of the modern animal rights movement, highlights a nasty paradox concerning vivisection – the dissection of live animals for purposes of research – and other forms of animal experimentation. Put simply, such experimentation appears to rest on two assumptions: its usefulness depends on the animals involved being similar to us; its morality depends on their being different. It should be possible to resolve the matter, one might suppose, simply by establishing whether or not (non-human) animals are like us. But actually things are much more complicated than this.

MOSQUITOES HAVE FEELINGS TOO?

Some animals are obviously much more like human beings than others. We bear little similarity to mosquitoes, snails and other invertebrates; in evolutionary terms, these are distant relatives and have little in common with us in the way they live or how their bodies work. Conducting experiments on or with such animals might further our understanding of crop pests, for instance, or the transmission of diseases, but it would not

TIMELINE

1871	1964
Charles Darwin's *The Descent of Man* argues that there is no basic difference between human beings and other animals	The treatment of research animals in the USA is regulated by the Animal Welfare Act

generally allow us to infer anything useful about how *our* bodies function. It is merely that the lifestyles of these animals impinge upon ours, so there are potential benefits from understanding them better.

These animals are obviously very different from us. We may ask, though, whether the fact that they are different makes it morally acceptable to carry out experiments on them. The fact of difference should not in itself carry any moral weight. Humans are different in all sorts of ways, but that fact does not entitle one individual or group to

Speciesism

The term 'speciesism' was coined by the Oxford-based psychologist Richard Ryder in 1970 to describe a form of discrimination based on species membership, exactly as racism and sexism are discrimination on the basis of race and sex. It is not necessarily 'speciesist' to treat species differently, any more than it is sexist to refuse males access to breast-screening. Rather, Ryder has in mind cases where the greater interests of non-human animals are overridden by human interests purely because the latter are human. To avoid the charge of prejudice, there must be some *morally* relevant reason for making such a distinction. It may be acceptable to swat a mosquito because it helps to spread malaria, or perhaps even because it gives an irritating bite, but not *simply* because it is a mosquito.

exploit other individuals or groups. If I am stronger or cleverer or richer or whiter than you, I am not thereby justified in shutting you up in a cage and conducting experiments on you.

Proponents of animal rights generally insist that the critical question in determining the moral consideration due to an animal is its level of consciousness – in particular, its capacity to experience pain and pleasure. It may be true that a mosquito, for instance, is less complex in its physical organization than a human being, but this fact alone does not tell us much about the animal's state of consciousness. The truth is that we do not have the *faintest* idea what it is like to be a mosquito or any other animal. Nor does it follow that so-called 'lower' animals experience things with less intensity than we do. Compared to people, dogs have a far more acute sense of smell

1970

Richard Ryder coins the term 'speciesism'

1986

In the UK, experiments involving vivisection are controlled by the Animals (Scientific Procedures) Act

Getting into animal minds

We may agree that the moral consideration due to animals should be determined by their capacity to experience pain and pleasure. But how on earth do we assess this capacity? If I see you hit your thumb with a hammer and hear you let out a loud shriek, I assume that your experience is the same as mine would be in the same circumstances: pain. This kind of analogy with our own experience is all we have to go on when it comes to understanding animals. Most mammals react to (what we would consider to be) painful stimuli in much the same way as we do – recoiling from a source of pain, emitting a range of shrieks and screams, etc. – so it is plausible to suppose that their subjective experience is similar too. We are on relatively safe ground in making such inferences about our close relatives, apes and monkeys, but the method of analogy is decidedly precarious when it comes to distant relatives, such as insects, slugs and jellyfishes. The truth is that we have absolutely no idea how such animals experience their world.

and many birds have sharper eyesight. It is reasonable to suppose that animals with a particularly acute sense suffer more if exposed to an especially intense and unpleasant stimulus to that sense.

NO FUNDAMENTAL DIFFERENCE

There are, on the other hand, some animals that are in certain respects very similar to human beings. As Ryder implies in the opening quotation, our whole understanding of animal species and their relationships has been revolutionized by Charles Darwin's theory of evolution by natural selection, which is accepted by all biologists as the foundation of their study. According to the theory, animal species are more or less closely related depending on how recently they share a common ancestor. On this basis, in order of increasingly close relatedness, humans are vertebrates (like fishes, reptiles and birds); mammals (like dogs, lions and sheep); and primates (like monkeys and apes). In general, we are more similar to our closer relatives both anatomically (in the structure of our bodies) and physiologically (in the way our bodies function).

Given these similarities, it is certainly plausible to claim that we can learn much about the functioning of human beings by studying our close relatives in the animal kingdom and carrying out experiments (including vivisection) on them. Indeed, it is undeniable that much *has* been learned in these ways. Much medical research, for instance, could not have been done without the use of monkeys and apes. But it is precisely the similarities that make these animals revealing subjects of experimentation that lead us to suppose that their conscious experience, including their feeling of pain, is similar to ours (*see box*). 'There is no fundamental difference,' Darwin writes, 'between man and the higher mammals in their mental faculties.' And if there is no fundamental difference in mental faculties – and here even Ryder's 'cruel experimenter' appears to be in agreement, implicitly at least – there should be no fundamental difference in moral consideration either.

THE ANIMAL AND HUMAN COST

It seems, then, that the cruel experimenter's argument collapses. Some animals are indeed very different from us, but others are very similar, and it is these latter that are likely to be most useful in experimentation aimed at giving insight into the way humans function. The closer the relative, apparently, the more useful and reliable the data that can be derived from experimenting on it – and following the cruel experimenter's logic, the more unethical such experimentation becomes.

> **SOME WILL TAKE REFUGE IN THE OLD CLICHÉ THAT HUMANS ARE DIFFERENT FROM OTHER ANIMALS. BUT WHEN DID A DIFFERENCE JUSTIFY A MORAL PREJUDICE?**
> Richard Ryder,
> animal rights pioneer, 1970

This line of reasoning does not make animal research wrong, but it emphasizes the point that we must weigh up the true benefits and costs (including the animal's suffering) and not hide behind specious arguments. It may be that the benefits, in terms of human health or prosperity, are sufficient to justify the costs, but it is important to realize that the price is paid not only by the animals involved but also by ourselves. Animal experimentation may allow us to live longer and more healthily, but our humanity does not ultimately depend on longevity or freedom from disease; the respect we show for other animals is a mark of our magnanimity as a species, and this is inevitably diminished when we show by our actions that we attach little value to their lives.

The condensed idea
Taking advantage of the relatives

40 Eating animals

Imagine life as a breeding sow. It isn't a long life – you'll probably be slaughtered before your fourth birthday. Still, you don't do much else but eat, so you have plenty of time to grow pretty enormous, perhaps up to 250 kilos (550 pounds). In spite of your size, you spend most of your days in a cramped metal-barred crate so narrow that you can't turn around, a concrete floor beneath your trotters. Perhaps five times in your life you are moved to another cramped stall, where you have a litter of piglets that are forever separated by bars and soon removed for incarceration or slaughter.

This is not just any sow – it is a factory-farmed sow. Conditions and regulations vary from country to country, of course, and some factory-farming regimes are worse than others. But such intensive farming methods always entail that pigs cannot do the kind of things that pigs like to do – socializing, wallowing in mud, rooting around in the soil for food, tending to their young. Instead, these highly intelligent animals spend a life of misery and frustration. And much the same goes for other intensively farmed animals, such as cows and chickens.

Some such methods are inevitable if the global demand for cheap meat and dairy products, currently running at hundreds of millions of tonnes a year, is to be met. So is it right that many billions of non-human animals live short and wretched lives in order to satisfy the human craving for meat?

TIMELINE

1st–2nd century AD	1859
Plutarch condemns the practice of eating meat	Charles Darwin's *On the Origin of Species* sets forth the theory of evolution by natural selection

NEED OR PLEASURE?

The assumption underlying human meat-eating is that other animals are inferior to, or less valuable than, humans; they are put on Earth only to serve human needs (*see page 153*). Such a view is still very widely held, though from a scientific perspective it is much harder to sustain in the light of Darwin's theory of evolution, which suggests that there is no essential difference between human and non-human animals and that they form part of a single continuum of life.

Nor is it true that humans *need* meat in their diet in order to flourish; testimony to this are the many millions of vegetarians in the world today. Indeed, from an ecological perspective, there is a strong case for saying that humans should *not* eat meat. The idea that intensive farming methods are a necessary response to the problem of feeding the world's growing population is the reverse of the truth. The process of converting food grown to feed factory-farm animals into meat results in the greater part of its energy value being lost. Eating plant food direct, rather than via the alimentary canals of meat-producing animals, would give us a better chance of feeding the rapidly growing number of human mouths.

It is hard, then, to justify eating meat produced by today's intensive farming methods – if you accept, that is, that animals such as pigs are intelligent animals that deserve at

Nature's way

It is sometimes suggested that predation is natural and hence that it is 'nature's way' for humans to eat meat. It is true that many animals, such as tigers and crocodiles, are naturally carnivorous, preying on other animals for their food, but what is natural for a tiger is not natural for a human, and it is generally agreed that the earliest humans were primarily plant-eaters. In any case, the fact that something is 'natural' does not necessarily mean that it is good or something we should try to emulate. Male lions follow their nature in killing a rival's offspring, but in human society such behaviour is generally frowned upon.

1860

Ralph Waldo Emerson sees vegetarianism as vital in the pursuit of moral perfection

2006

Global consumption of pork approaches 100 million tonnes

Man on the menu

Today there is a strong taboo against cannibalism, but it has not always been so. Throughout human history, the practice of humans eating the flesh of other humans has been widespread, often as a kind of ritual observance and even as a form of food. The vision of human corpses hanging in butchers' shops understandably fills us with revulsion, but the problem here is at least partly the demonstrable lack of respect (a point we should consider when we see non-human animals dangling from butchers' hooks). Many people wish to get closer to nature, to live as integral members of a broader ecology. What could be more natural than to recycle our bodies by entering the food chain? It is not obvious what would be actually *wrong* with such a practice, provided that it was performed with all due respect – and with the donor/dinner's consent, of course.

least minimally humane treatment. The only sure basis on which to build a defence, perhaps, is the undeniable truth that many humans enjoy consuming meat. The question then is whether the pleasure gained from tasting flesh is sufficient to justify the amount of suffering caused to the original owners of that flesh. Many feel that the answer to this has to be 'no', and the more conscientious among them change their habits accordingly.

SHOULD PIGS BE GRATEFUL FOR BACON?

But what of the food animals (admittedly a small minority) that are kept in relatively humane conditions? It is reasonable to suppose that such animals, given freedom to move about and behave as they choose, lead generally pleasant lives. Provided that their slaughter is both unforeseen and painless, is there any objection to our eating their meat? Indeed, these animals would not exist at all were it not for the value of their flesh – they are bred specifically to produce meat – so is it not a good thing for the animals themselves that our taste for meat gives them an opportunity to live happy (albeit curtailed) lives?

Most people probably feel that a short, happy life is better than no life at all. Many of us, of course, end up living such lives, usually without knowing it in advance. This seems to be very much the situation of animals kept in free-range conditions. It makes a difference, though, if the end of life is deliberately brought about. We might rejoice that the life of someone murdered at an early age was happy; however, we would say that although they lived well, their life ended badly and too soon: the manner of their death was wrong, in part because the previous happiness was not allowed to continue. In a similar way the interests of a free-range animal – in particular, its interest in continuing to lead a contented life – are damaged (terminally) by its killing. It may be that the animal would not have existed at all but for our liking for its flesh, but our creating something does not give us the right to terminate it. We usually choose to bring babies into the world but are not allowed to change our minds once we have done so.

> **FOR THE SAKE OF SOME LITTLE MOUTHFUL OF FLESH, WE DEPRIVE A SOUL OF THE SUN AND LIGHT, AND OF THAT PROPORTION OF LIFE AND TIME IT HAD BEEN BORN INTO THE WORLD TO ENJOY.**
>
> Plutarch, Greek essayist, 1st–2nd century AD

CARNIVOROUS OSTRICHES

All that can be said with safety is that it is *better* to eat humanely produced meat than the products of factory farms. The explanation, though not the justification, for our readiness to eat the latter is often a sort of wilful ignorance. We may be vaguely aware of what the processes of production involve – but perhaps not as vaguely as we would wish, and we take pains not to find out more. A consciousness of guilt may linger, nevertheless. As the American essayist Ralph Waldo Emerson observed: 'However scrupulously the slaughterhouse is concealed in the graceful distance of miles, there is complicity.'

The condensed idea
The rights and wrongs of meat

41 The sanctity of life

Medicine and the biological sciences have taken enormous strides over the past century. This progress has given practitioners an unprecedented ability to control human destinies, not least to exercise significant control over matters of life and death. But the fact that lives can be prolonged and deaths postponed does not necessarily mean that the extra life gained is valuable or worth living.

Today, people generally live many years longer than they did a century ago; diseases that were once a death sentence are now routinely cured; babies that would never once have reached full term can now survive for decades. But severely damaged babies inevitably take a heavy toll on those who care for them; and for the elderly and infirm, living longer isn't always living better. We have become adept at prolonging life though we are not always so good at putting a proper value on it. Is a life always worth living, or is it sometimes better to bring it to an end?

SANCTITY VERSUS QUALITY OF LIFE

In some religious traditions, life – human life, at any rate – is sacrosanct. According to Christian teaching, life is a gift from God; each body is the physical temple of the soul, an immaterial spirit that is the innermost aspect of our being. To bring a life to an end is to 'play God', in the sense that by doing so we take upon ourselves a prerogative that belongs only to the one who created us. It is sinful, then, not to respect the 'sanctity of life', to show ingratitude to God by failing to cherish the priceless gift he has bestowed upon us.

TIMELINE

1973	1981
The *Roe v. Wade* ruling by the US Supreme Court upholds the right to abortion until viability (when the embryo is able to survive outside the uterus)	The first embryonic stem cells are derived from mouse embryos

Taking a secular perspective, many philosophers reject the idea that life is intrinsically valuable, or good in itself; they believe, rather, that there are sometimes circumstances in which it would be better to bring a life to an end. In reaching decisions of this kind, the autonomy of the individual is usually paramount: each person is generally presumed to be in the best position to assess the value of their own life and hence to decide, ultimately, if theirs is a life worth living.

PRO-CHOICE OR PRO-LIFE

Religious convictions often exacerbate the dispute between those who support abortion ('pro-choice') and those who oppose it ('pro-life'). The main bone of contention between them is the moral status given to the embryo. At the time of birth, it is (few would dispute) a distinct person with basic rights and interests that deserve full moral consideration; most would say that to kill a baby at full term is wrong. But when does the embryo attain the status of being a person, in the sense of having rights and interests, and how are these rights and interests to be weighed against those of the mother?

The Christian, and more particularly Catholic, view is that an embryo is endowed with a soul at the point of conception, and it is having a soul that makes it a person worthy of moral consideration. From this perspective, there is never a point at which the mother's interests can 'trump' those of the embryo: termination of the embryo is never permissible; abortion is murder.

Embryonic stem cells

The question of how much moral consideration we should give to human life at its earliest stages is raised by the use of embryonic stem cells in research. These cells are 'totipotent', which means that they can develop into any of the body's many different, specialized cell types. The ultimate aim is to transplant these cells into injured parts of the body, such as the brain or spinal cord, where they would develop and permanently replace damaged cells. The early-stage embryos from which these cells are obtained are destroyed in the harvesting process, however, so this kind of research is seen by some critics as no less morally objectionable than abortion.

1993	1994
Physician-assisted suicide (PAS) is decriminalized in the Netherlands	The Death with Dignity Act, allowing PAS, is approved in Oregon, USA

A biologist, by contrast, understands human gestation as a gradual process of development over time. There is no one point where an embryo can be said to turn from a collection of dividing cells into a human being. For the first two weeks the embryo is a ball of cells with no central nervous system, so there is no possibility that it has any consciousness of pain. At this time it cannot properly be said to have an individual identity and indeed may still develop into two (or four) distinct embryos. From this point the embryo gradually develops, as the brain and spinal cord, then the limbs, become increasingly apparent. The value we attach to the embryo is also incremental, growing as the inchoate life moves closer to a recognizably human form and 'personhood'. In countries where abortion is permitted, this developmental understanding is usually reflected in legislation that is more permissive of early termination. As the embryo develops, in other words, its interests are increasingly given priority over those of the mother.

DYING WITH DIGNITY?

The idea that human life is sacrosanct and to be protected at all costs is no less relevant in the matter of euthanasia, where life that is already underway is brought to an end. Indeed, the distinction between euthanasia and abortion need not be very great. Unless particular importance is attached to the fact of birth – an event that in itself appears morally insignificant – one who supports abortion of a late-term foetus whose life prospects are extremely poor cannot, with consistency, oppose the killing (in effect, neonatal euthanasia) of a newborn baby with similar prospects.

The most significant difference, in the case of euthanasia, is that it may be voluntary. A patient, typically someone with a terminal condition and suffering pain that can no longer be adequately managed by drugs, may feel that her life is no longer worth living and request assistance in bringing it to a painless and (what she regards as) dignified end. The usual liberal position here is that the state has no business to interfere with the considered views of its citizens in matters that do no harm to others; in such cases, an individual's autonomy – her right to make decisions that affect the course of her own life – should be paramount and her wishes respected.

One common objection to voluntary euthanasia is simply that the active taking of life is incompatible with a doctor's role and purpose: to cure and

Slippery slopes

Perhaps the commonest objection raised against voluntary euthanasia is that it represents the first step on a perilously slippery slope: allowing one (arguably) acceptable practice – physician-assisted suicide carried out at the request of the patient – will lead inexorably to other more obnoxious practices such as non-voluntary euthanasia. There is nothing inevitable about this descent, however. The crucial point about voluntary euthanasia is patient consent. Complications arise, certainly, when patients lose the ability to give consent, and safeguards need to be put in place to make sure that the system is not abused. Such things as living wills suggest a way forward, but perhaps adequate safeguards cannot be devised and the practice should remain illegal, as it is today in most countries. But this is a purely practical consideration with no clear implications for other forms of euthanasia. A separate argument can be made for non-voluntary euthanasia, for instance in the case of individuals in a persistent vegetative state. Still, such practices should be considered on their own merits – there is no compelling reason to see them at the foot of a slippery slope.

care for patients. It is true that killing has never been part of the description of what a doctor does, but this says nothing about what a doctor *should* do. Certainly we should respect a doctor's autonomy no less than that of her patient, and there should not be any pressure or obligation to carry out euthanasia if her conscience suggests that she should not. But, again, this says nothing of the doctor who sees no conflict between her duties and a request for euthanasia.

This aside, the principal objections to voluntary euthanasia are practical ones, questioning whether adequate safeguards can be put in place to prevent abuse (*see box above*). By focusing on practicalities, critics may appear to concede that euthanasia performed with the full agreement of the patient is justified, in specific cases at least. If this is so, the task becomes to establish guidelines sufficiently rigorous that permissible and impermissible cases can be distinguished.

The condensed idea
Valuing life, curtailing life

42 Death

Timor mortis conturbat me ('Fear of death troubles me'). The refrain of William Dunbar's famous lament captures a universal truth: nothing in life concerns us so much as the ending of it. We live constantly in the shadow of death, and much of what we do and think is coloured by the fact that our lives are finite and will inevitably end sooner or later.

A universal truth, perhaps, but not at all clear. For the word 'death' has two quite distinct meanings. The death that we all finally meet is an event, or more precisely a process, that brings life to an end. And while death in this sense – the process of dying – is, by definition, the termination of life, it is very much part of life too: there is no doubt that it is something that befalls us when we are (still) alive. 'Death' may also, however, refer to the state or condition that we are in after death, in the first sense, has terminated our lives; or – again, more precisely – it may describe a state in which there is no 'we', because the beings that we once were no longer exist.

Should we be afraid of death? Is it rational to have such a fear? These questions mean very different things, depending on whether we mean the process of dying or the state of being dead. There is nothing irrational about fearing the process of dying, the final episode in our lives. We may die suddenly and painlessly in our sleep, but, unfortunately, dying is often a nasty, painful and undignified business. Some people may be more stoical than others when faced with the prospect of an unpleasant death, but it is clearly something that might reasonably make anyone feel apprehensive.

TIMELINE

4th century BC	4th–3rd century BC	c.1500
Plato argues that the soul survives the death of the body	Epicurus maintains that death should hold no fear for us	Scottish poet William Dunbar writes *The Lament for the Makaris*

Banishing the shadow of death

'So unsure is men's judgment that they are unable to determine even death itself.' So wrote the Roman author Pliny the Elder in the first century AD, and in some respects the problem is with us still. Death is often defined negatively, as the extinction of life, and this involves the irreversible cessation of the processes and functions that sustain life. Among these various processes, arrest of the blood circulation has, historically, been regarded as especially significant. Today, however, the expert consensus is that the crucial factor is brain death – specifically, irreversible loss of function in critical parts of the brain stem. Dramatic progress in medicine's capacity to maintain or prolong 'life' – or rather, to postpone the failure of many of the functions that normally sustain it – has meant that brain death may often occur *before* other vital processes have ceased. The gruesome consequence of this, in today's intensive-care units, is the so-called 'beating-heart cadaver'. A proper ethical response to such cases, as well as to related issues such as the timing of organ removal for transplantation, requires that we allow modern scientific insights to dispel much of the mystery and superstition that have long surrounded the process of dying.

But what of the state of being dead? Or having ceased to exist? Or having ended our life on Earth? Some people believe that the end of our terrestrial existence is a point of transition to some kind of afterlife – another life that may be better or worse than our life on Earth and is certainly different from it. Others, without religious or spiritual belief, think of dying as the end of life, plain and simple, and feel that beyond death nothing awaits us except physical annihilation. The implications of the view you take on this matter could hardly be greater.

HOPE AND FEAR, HEAVEN AND HELL

Clearly, believing that life on Earth is not all there is – that there is some kind of afterlife – may give grounds for fear or hope, depending on what is to be expected after death. Many cultures suppose that we have a spiritual component – a soul – that survives the death of our physical body. The

1932

Bertolt Brecht's play *The Mother* is first performed in Berlin

1979

Thomas Nagel discusses, in *Mortal Questions*, whether death harms us ancient Egyptians performed complex rituals to prepare the dead for the afterlife; Plato believed that the soul existed before and after the physical demise of the body; and modern Hindus, Christians, Jews and Muslims all have elaborate beliefs about post-mortem survival.

In each case, there is an explicit connection between the quality of an individual's terrestrial life and the fate that awaits him or her in the hereafter. Thus Hindus, for instance, suppose that each individual undergoes repeated rebirths, the length and form of which are determined by their *karma* – effectively the balance sheet of their good and bad deeds performed in former incarnations. Christianity and Islam, on the other hand, have elaborate visions of heaven and hell, where individuals are rewarded and punished for their behaviour on Earth. For followers of these religions, the prospect of life beyond terrestrial death, giving reasons for both fear and hope, is likely to have the profoundest influence on their moral outlook during their time on Earth.

CARPE DIEM, QUAM MINIMUM CREDULA POSTERO ("SEIZE THE DAY, TRUSTING AS LITTLE AS POSSIBLE IN THE NEXT").

Horace, Roman poet, first century BC

IS DEATH BAD FOR US?

Should people who do not believe in an afterlife fear death? Does it make sense to entertain fears about a future state of the world in which one simply does not exist? A famous argument to show that such fear was misplaced was made by the Greek philosopher Epicurus. Though death is regarded as 'the most awful of evils', he argues that it should in fact mean 'nothing to us, seeing that, when we are, death is not come, and when death is come, we are not': in other words, it cannot touch us because we have ceased to exist and cannot therefore be harmed – and it is foolish to fear something that cannot harm us. Indeed, he argues, the time after we have died is no different from the time before we were born; we are indifferent to the latter, and so should we be to the former.

Not everyone is convinced by Epicurus' argument. The US philosopher Thomas Nagel and others argue that death is bad for us because it damages our interests. It is not the case, we may concede, that the state of being dead or non-existent is bad in itself – that is not what makes death bad. It is bad because it prevents our having various good things that we would have had if we had not died; we are worse off than we would otherwise have been because some of our central desires are inevitably left unrealized, some of the projects and plans that give value to our lives left unfinished.

Death, then, is harmful because it is a curtailment of life and thus a deprivation of good things. It is for this reason that we take a different view of the time before our birth and the time after our death. The former, unlike the latter, does not deprive us of anything – we are not 'cut off' from enjoying things that we might otherwise have had. By the same token, of course, death may do us good, by preventing us from suffering bad things that we would have suffered if we had lived.

LIVE LIFE

If this is the kind of harm done by death, the best way to reduce the damage is to die later. We might well manage this – by living healthier lives, for instance, and taking fewer risks – but these are matters of prudence, not morality. Beyond such prudential considerations, there may be nothing we can do to influence the time of our death. To the extent that it is pointless to concern ourselves with things that are beyond our control, it may be that Epicurus is right after all. If death is an inevitable deprivation of good things, regret, rather than fear, might be a more appropriate response to it. Indeed, best of all would be to follow the advice of the ever-optimistic title character of Bertolt Brecht's play *The Mother*: 'Don't be afraid of death so much as an inadequate life.' We should live life to the full, making the most of the opportunities that life gives us and attending more to what we do than what we leave undone.

The condensed idea
Facing death:
transition or oblivion?

43 Genetic engineering

Everything about us is affected by the genes we inherit from our parents. The way we function and behave is determined, to some degree, by information encoded in the chemical deoxyribonucleic acid (DNA) – the 'molecule of life' – located within the cells that make up our bodies. Ever-expanding knowledge of genetic processes has been enhanced by the discovery of techniques that allow scientists to manipulate, or 'engineer', the information carried by DNA. The capacity to influence or control such things as intelligence and appearance – and perhaps even to clone whole individuals – opens up the possibility of human beings 'playing God' as never before.

We are sometimes said to be the products of our genes: we are the way we are because we are constituted according to a blueprint laid down by our DNA. This kind of genetic determinism is certainly exaggerated. We are also the products of the environment in which we develop: our personality, talents and much else about us are shaped by cultural influences, by the kind of education we receive, and so on. We are the way we are, in reality, as a consequence of a complex interaction between innumerable biological and environmental factors. There is little consensus, however, on the respective roles of biology and environment – of nature and nurture, as it is sometimes put – in this interaction.

TIMELINE

1973

The first genetically modified animal – a mouse – is created

1993

Research into the genetic basis of sexuality leads to press reports of a 'gay gene'

GAY GENES, FAT GENES, CRIME GENES ...

Newspaper editors are fond of stories about genetic breakthroughs: the discovery of a 'gay gene' that explains homosexuality, or a 'fat gene' that determines obesity. Such reports are usually wildly simplistic, but do they contain a germ of truth? Much of morality is concerned with what we should and shouldn't do; if I say that something is wrong and you shouldn't do it, I imply that it is possible for you to refrain from doing it. But if you are gay because your genes have made you so, it doesn't make much sense to say that it is right or wrong. You were destined to be gay from the moment of your conception, when a unique combination of genes from your parents made you the person you are. If gay genes make you gay, nobody can be held responsible for that fact – except perhaps God, if he made the genes in the first place.

It isn't necessary to believe in full-blown determinism to think that insights into our genetic make-up might require an adjustment of our moral attitudes. For instance, a number of studies have suggested that the probability of engaging in anti-social and criminal behaviour is increased if a particular gene, or combination of genes, is present. Such claims remain highly controversial, but if they were confirmed, current attitudes and assumptions would be bound to change. If it became possible to identify potential offenders in advance, it might be that their propensity to offend could be reduced or eliminated by some kind of genetic, perhaps drug-based, therapy. More ominously, there is a danger that people found to have a certain genetic profile would be labelled as troublemakers in advance of their doing wrong. While it might not be appropriate to blame or punish such people for their (potential) bad behaviour, it might still be necessary to imprison them to protect others. And if their tendency to criminality were found to be 'hardwired' into them by their genes, we might have to temper any optimism that programmes of reform and rehabilitation would do much to change them.

2003

The complete sequencing of the human genome is announced

2007

The FTO gene ('fat gene') is linked with obesity in humans

A rich man's game

Perhaps only one thing is certain to remain true of human genetic engineering: it is never going to be cheap. Techniques will be streamlined and efficiencies made, but it is bound to remain expensive. If designing babies becomes a reality, it is sure to be a rich man's game. Only the wealthy will be able to escape the vagaries of unassisted sexual reproduction; they alone will enjoy the privilege of endowing their progeny with advantages that set them apart from the unwashed masses. *Plus ça change.* Purely on the basis of cost, the business of genetic engineering is sure to offend those who have an egalitarian view of social justice.

MANIPULATING GENOMES

Since the 1970s an increasingly sophisticated set of techniques has been developed that allow an organism to be modified by directly manipulating its genome (that is, all of its genetic material, considered as a whole). Genes can be removed, or new DNA introduced, in such a way that the physical form and characteristics of the organism are altered in some desirable way: a plant may acquire resistance to a particular pest, for instance, or a mosquito may develop an internal environment that is inhospitable to the malarial parasite it usually carries.

At the current rate of progress it will not be long before extensive modification of the human genome becomes technically possible. To take only the most-publicized example, techniques are likely to be developed that allow parents not only to choose the sex of their prospective offspring but also to determine, or at least influence, various desirable characteristics, such as their intelligence, aptitudes and physical appearance. But is it right that parents exercise such power?

DESIGNING BABIES

It is probable that gene therapies will soon be available to prevent children from inheriting from their parents a number of highly debilitating diseases. Many would accept a parent's right to make use of such means, yet baulk at the idea of essentially similar methods being used to increase the probability that a child might be, say, of higher-than-average intelligence. Both attributes – being healthy and being clever – are basically good for the child and likely to improve its life prospects. Promoting the interests of their child seems to be just the sort of thing that parents should do. So what makes genetic intervention acceptable in one case (preventing illness) and not in the other (enhancing intelligence)?

One objection to the idea of a child concocted according to its parents' wishlist lies precisely in the unbalanced relationship that it implies between the two sides. Much of our value as human beings resides in our individuality, much of our self-esteem in our sense of autonomy and independence from others; each person is, or should be – in the old phrase – 'his own man', independent in thought and action. All this is undermined by the idea that we are as we are because someone else has decided how we should be: human dignity demands more than this.

Accepting the chance combinations of sexual reproduction, parents normally love their children simply because they are their own; they love them unconditionally. But what if there is a 'blueprint' – what if they have drawn up an advance specification for their child – and the child fails to match the design brief? A burden of expectation will be laid on the shoulders of a 'designer baby', and in the end it is most likely to be the child itself that will suffer. Either it will cause disappointment by failing to live up to expectations or – if it *does* meet those expectations – it truly will have been designed and thus deprived of the independence that is so central to our dignity as human beings.

The condensed idea
Designing babies

44 Cloning

With due respect to history's other celebrated sheep, none has left as significant a mark as Dolly. At her birth, on July 5, 1996, Dolly became the first clone, or genetic copy, of an adult mammal. The announcement of her birth in February the following year sparked a storm of fevered debate over the future implications of cloning, including – most controversially – the prospect that the new technique might be used to produce human clones.

Dolly was produced by a method known as somatic (body) cell nuclear transfer, or SCNT, which was pioneered by the British embryologist Ian Wilmut and his research team at the Roslin Institute near Edinburgh, Scotland. Wilmut took an unfertilized egg cell from a Blackface ewe, removed its nucleus, and replaced it with the nucleus of a body cell extracted from a six-year-old Finnish Dorset ewe. The resulting embryo was then implanted in the womb of a surrogate ewe, which, some five months later, gave birth to Dolly. As almost all an animal's DNA is located in the cell nucleus, the illustrious lamb was, genetically, a near-identical copy of the Finnish Dorset from which the nucleus was taken. Dolly was, in effect, the identical twin of one of its two donor mothers.

Dolly was not the first cloned mammal – others had been produced in the decade before her birth with the use of embryonic cells. But she was the first to be produced by taking somatic (body) cells from an adult animal – cells that had already differentiated into the many separate types that make

Saviour siblings

Cells or organs taken from a clone would be a perfect match for those of the donor and so could be used to treat illnesses in the latter without fear of rejection – the body's usual immune response to the presence of foreign tissue. Bone-marrow cells from a clone should, for instance, be highly effective in treating a child with leukaemia. However, the current use of such 'saviour siblings', specifically bred to provide relatively closely (though not perfectly) matched cells and tissues, is already highly controversial, as it seems to contravene the fundamental (Kantian) moral prohibition against using people as a means to something else and not as an end in themselves. The issue is explored by Kazuo Ishiguro in his 2005 novel *Never Let Me Go*, in which cloned children are produced with the express intention of providing a bank of organs as spare parts for non-clones, or 'normals'. Such a scenario is extreme, however, as a more realistic and less repugnant possibility is that cloning techniques could be used to generate tissues or organs without creating whole people or foetuses.

up a mature body. It was one of Dolly's achievements to show that this process of differentiation could be reversed and hence that genetic copies of adult animals could be made. While Wilmut and his team were primarily interested in the possible agricultural uses of cloning, they were aware that their methodology would have medical applications, especially in the area of human reproduction, and could in principle be extended to the cloning of human beings. Predictably, it is this last aspect that has provoked the most intense ethical debate.

BLOOD TIES AND IMMORTALITY

Blood has always been thicker than water. Every human society has attached great significance to the blood connections – the genetic links – that exist between relatives and family members. Cloning might offer an alternative means by which infertile or homosexual couples could have genetically related offspring. The procedure would involve taking a body cell from one or

1996

Dolly the sheep becomes the first clone of an adult mammal

2005

Kazuo Ishiguro's *Never Let Me Go* gives a dystopian view of organ farming

Dino-cloning

Could cloning be used to bring extinct animals back to life? This is the inspiration for Michael Crichton's 1990 science-fiction novel *Jurassic Park*. The book, brought to cinemas three years later by Steven Spielberg, features an amusement park populated by dinosaurs cloned from DNA recovered from the blood of fossilized mosquitoes. The prospects of replicating animals extinct for millions of years are dim, as the DNA – even supposing that it could be obtained at all – would probably be hopelessly degraded. However, there is an intriguing possibility that cloning techniques could be used to replicate recently extinct animals or to help preserve severely threatened species.

other partner, and the resulting child would be a near-identical copy of the donor. Some critics complain that too much significance is attached to genetic relationship and that there might be a negative social impact, for instance on the current practice of adoption. Others suggest that the desire to have genetically related offspring is deep-seated and that – unless there are compelling reasons that indicate otherwise – people are entitled to receive assistance of this kind.

One intriguing aspect of cloning – at least in the minds of science-fiction writers – is the prospect it offers of duplicating individuals, especially loved ones who have died. The novelty of such an idea has tended to obscure its obvious limitations. It may be true that cells taken from a deceased child, for instance, could be used to produce a genetic replica, but the clone would clearly be a distinct person with a distinct personality. To suppose otherwise is to exaggerate the role of genetics in determining personality and to ignore the huge part played by cultural factors. The point becomes obvious if one considers 'replacing' a beloved 70-year-old grandfather – a unique individual shaped by a lifetime's experience – with a newborn baby, albeit one sharing the same DNA.

A variant of this view is the idea that individuals could achieve a certain kind of immortality – or at least an extension of life – by having *themselves* cloned. This hope is entirely groundless, just as it would be to suppose that being survived by an identical twin would prolong one's own life.

IDENTITY ANGST AND CLONISM

There are doubts whether cloning by means of nuclear transfer will ever be sufficiently safe or efficient to be of practical use in human reproduction. It took over 200 unsuccessful attempts to produce Dolly, and the rates of stillbirth and birth abnormality encountered in the procedure are extremely high. But many objections have also been raised on matters of principle.

One area of concern is the psychological problems that a clone might face in coming to terms with her own identity and her peculiar familial and social relationships. A cloned individual would certainly find herself in uncharted waters. None of us has had to deal with a situation in which one of those responsible for parenting us is a sort of genetic twin separated in age by several decades. The belief that we are the products of our genes may be unfounded, but it is pervasive, and a clone is likely to be affected by the knowledge that she has a genetic double who has already lived much of a life: someone who has followed a particular path, achieved things and made mistakes, and suffered various medical conditions, some perhaps due to genetic factors. It is difficult enough for young people to establish their own sense of identity – a sense of their own unique place in the world – so the additional pressures felt by a clone could only make matters worse.

A clone's anxiety about her own status and individuality is likely to be mirrored in society as a whole, some members of which are usually quick to form prejudicial attitudes towards subgroups that are different in some way. In some cultures, twins have been subject to taboo, and there is a danger that such atavistic suspicions might resurface in the case of clones. Such discrimination, or 'clonism', would be based on a perception that a genetic copy was somehow inferior to the original – in some sense less valuable than a 'full' person – and it is likely that such negative attitudes would reinforce a clone's own anxieties about her individuality.

The condensed idea
Standing on the
shoulders of sheep

War

'War is the continuation of politics by other means.' If Karl von Clausewitz's famous observation is correct, military conflict seems certain to remain a permanent aspect of the human condition. For humans are political animals, forever hungry for power and land and other resources that are necessarily limited. It is inevitable, therefore, that there will be disputes about which group lives where and which group tells others what to do. Often these disputes will be beyond resolution by peaceful means and violent conflict will ensue.

V iews may differ on whether or not war is woven into the fabric of human nature, with some clinging doggedly to the hope that a future without warfare is possible. Few would disagree, however, that some disputes are worse than others and that not all violence is equally bad. 'War is an ugly thing,' wrote the Victorian philosopher John Stuart Mill, 'but not the ugliest of things: the decayed and degraded state of moral and patriotic feeling which thinks that nothing is *worth* a war, is much worse.' Mill, though clearly a man of peace himself, nevertheless believed that occasionally it is necessary to fight the good fight. Sometimes the cause may be so important that recourse to arms is the lesser of two evils: war may be just war.

THE SIX CONDITIONS OF JUST WAR

The idea of just war has a long history that extends back to St Augustine and the early Christian fathers. Originally founded on the moral obligation to seek justice and defend the innocent, the doctrine came in time to embody

TIMELINE

5th or 4th century BC	5th century AD	13th century
Sun Tzu writes *The Art of War*, the world's first work of military theory	St Augustine develops the Christian doctrine of just war	Thomas Aquinas refines the principles of just war

a central distinction between *jus ad bellum* ('justice in the move to war', the conditions under which it is morally right to take up arms) and *jus in bello* ('justice in war', rules of conduct once fighting is underway). These ideas provide the main structure of modern just war theory, which seeks to determine the circumstances that must exist and the criteria that must be met before war is justified. According to this theory, six conditions are recognized that must be jointly satisfied before it is considered right to initiate a war: just cause, right intention, proper authority, prospect of success, proportionality and last resort.

The first and most important of these conditions is **just cause**. Today, in Western countries, the scope of this condition is generally limited to defence against aggression. This includes, uncontroversially, self-defence against a violation of a country's basic rights – an attack on its political sovereignty and territorial integrity. More contentiously, it may be extended to cover assistance given to another country suffering such aggression. In earlier times, just cause was often religious in origin – a kind of justification that would generally be dismissed, in the secular West, as ideologically motivated. However, among adherents of religious fundamentalisms, resurgent in recent decades, a religious motive would be regarded as a prime (perhaps the sole) justification for going to war.

Just cause is not enough on its own. It must be accompanied by **right intention**. The sole motivation behind any action must be to right the wrong

Fighting God's good war

The origins of modern just war theory can be traced back to St Augustine, in the fifth century AD, who wrote in *The City of God* that it was 'the injustice of the opponent that lays on the wise man the duty of waging war ... The commandment forbidding killing was not broken by those who have waged war on the authority of God.' Augustine's ideas were refined in the 13th century by Thomas Aquinas, who was responsible for the hallowed distinction between *jus ad bellum* (defining the conditions under which it is morally right to take up arms) and *jus in bello* (defining the rules of conduct to be observed in the course of fighting).

1832

Karl von Clausewitz's highly influential *On War* is published

1862

The American Civil War prompts John Stuart Mill to extol the notion of just war

Steering a middle course

A just war may be fought unjustly, an unjust war justly: it is one thing, in other words, to embark on a war for the right reasons, another to conduct oneself in a morally appropriate manner once the fighting has started. This second aspect (*jus in bello*, according to usual terminology) encompasses a wide range of issues, including the use of particular types of weapons (nuclear, chemical, mines, scatter bombs, etc.) and the behaviour of individual soldiers in their relation both to the enemy and to civilians. One crucial point is **proportionality**: the means chosen to achieve a particular end must be proportionate. Most, for instance, would consider no military objective sufficiently important to justify a nuclear attack. A second point is **discrimination**: every effort must be made to distinguish combatants and non-combatants. It is generally considered immoral, for example, to target civilians, however effective it might be in military terms. The aerial bombardment of cities, by both Axis and Allied bombers, in the Second World War is often given as a case of such illicit failure to discriminate. A paradox here is that if the cause is compelling enough – if the evil to be averted is sufficiently great – it would seem to justify whatever means are necessary. Or so at least Winston Churchill believed when he said, 'There is no middle course in wartime.'

that was created by the original act of aggression or other cause. The claimed just cause cannot be a fig-leaf for some ulterior motive, such as national interest or territorial expansion.

A further condition is that a decision to take up arms is made by the **proper authority**. For most of human history, war was, as the poet John Dryden observed in the 17th century, 'the trade of kings'. In the following century, however, the French Revolution ensured that the right to declare war was transferred to whatever body or institution of the state held sovereign power. The concept of proper authority raises thorny questions about legitimate government and the appropriate relationship between decision-makers and people. For instance, the Nazi government of 1930s Germany clearly enjoyed sovereign power, but most would say that it lacked not only just cause but also basic legitimacy to declare and wage war.

A country should resort to war, even a just one, only if it has a reasonable **prospect of success**: there is generally no point in sacrificing lives and resources in vain. Some, though, would argue that it is right (and certainly not wrong) to resist an aggressor, however futile the gesture may be. Furthermore, a sense of **proportionality** must be observed. There must be a balance between the desired end and the likely consequences of getting there: the expected good, in terms of righting the wrong that constitutes the just cause, must be weighed against the anticipated damage, in terms of casualties, human suffering and so on.

> **POLITICS IS WAR WITHOUT BLOODSHED WHILE WAR IS POLITICS WITH BLOODSHED.**
>
> Mao Zedong, Chinese communist leader, 1938

'To subdue the enemy without a fight is the supreme excellence,' according to the Chinese general Sun Tzu, the world's first great military theorist. Military action must always be the **last resort** and is only ever justified if every other peaceful, non-military option has failed. As the British politician Tony Benn once pointed out, there is a sense in which 'all war represents a failure of diplomacy'.

The condensed idea
Politics by other means

46 Realpolitik

'Might is right' sounds like the morality of the jungle or the playground bully. Yet it could equally be the slogan of political realism, or realpolitik – arguably the most influential and pervasive theory explaining how and why states interact with one another as they do. Following the dictates of realpolitik, security and self-interest are the sole concerns a state should consider in determining its policies towards others. States secure their interests by exercising their power, while conflict – the natural dynamic of international relations – is the means by which power is gained and increased.

The guiding spirit of realpolitik is pragmatism; herein lies the reality of political realism. It might be nice, in an ideal world, if ethical concerns influenced the behaviour of states. But just look around: in the real world national interest trumps morality every time. This makes it sound as if realpolitik is offering a description, not a prescription – saying how things are, not how they should be. But political realists, of the classical variety at least, typically believe that the struggle for power and domination is rooted in human nature and hence that it is pointless to wish or suggest that things should be other than they are.

THE WEAKER MUST BOW DOWN TO THE STRONGER

The word 'realpolitik' (German for 'political realism') is relatively new – it was coined in the mid-19th century – but the attitudes and assumptions that underlie it are very much older. Doubtless the most famous political realist is

TIMELINE

5th century BC	1532	1938
Thucydides expresses realist attitudes in his *History of the Peloponnesian War*	Niccolò Machiavelli's *The Prince* gives a classic account of realist 'power politics'	British and French appeasement of Nazis at Munich symbolizes the failure of idealism

the Florentine Niccolò Machiavelli, who argues that conventional morality must be set aside in the interests of effective government, but he is himself picking up a tradition that can be traced back to ancient Greece.

In his account of the Peloponnesian War, written over 2,400 years ago, the Greek historian Thucydides writes a speech for a party of Athenian envoys, who are attempting, on the eve of conflict, to dissuade the Spartans from making a stand against their aggressive imperialism. Explaining their decision to hold on to their empire, Thucydides' Athenians speak precisely the language of realpolitik:

> In this we are constrained by three of the most powerful motives: honour, fear and self-interest. Nor are we the first to act in this way – it has always been the way that the weaker must bow down to the stronger. We feel that we are worthy of our power, as did you Spartans, until thought of your own interest made you speak of right and wrong. Talk of justice never deterred anyone from seizing by force whatever he could.

Safer to be feared than loved

Historically, the most celebrated realist is the Florentine political theorist Niccolò Machiavelli, who in *The Prince* (1532) famously counsels rulers that it is better to be feared than loved and that effective use of power depends on their readiness to disregard conventional morality. Like his 20th-century successors, Machiavelli makes a powerful case against the idealism of his contemporaries: 'Many have pictured republics and principalities which in fact have never been known or seen, because how one lives is so far distant from how one ought to live, that he who neglects what is done for what ought to be done, sooner effects his ruin than his preservation.'

FROM IDEALISM TO REALISM

The emergence of political realism in the 20th century was largely a reaction to the failures of what had gone before. Between the world wars, the dominant perspective on global politics was idealism, a somewhat utopian approach based on the assumption that war could be averted by establishing

1939

E. H. Carr gives an early expression of the modern realist outlook in *The Twenty Years' Crisis, 1919–1939*

1979

Kenneth Waltz develops the neorealist approach in his *Theory of International Politics*

effective international laws and organizations. The inadequacy of this view was cruelly exposed by the demise of idealism's showpiece, the League of Nations, and the naked aggression of Hitler and other fascist leaders.

Understandably in the circumstances, the generation of political realists who emerged during and after the Second World War shared a rather pessimistic view of the nature and conduct of international relations. The primary concern of statesmen, in their view, was the national interest, power the means of securing it; hence the struggle to win power was the driving force of political activity. These early ('classical') realists believed that power could be increased only at the expense of other states: there would always be winners and losers in the interplay of states, and so the business of satisfying national interests (by winning greater power) was necessarily a matter of competition and conflict. And because they thought that the struggle for power was a more or less immutable aspect of human nature, they held out little prospect of change in the future. Conflict and war were inevitable: the task of the analyst was limited to assessing how they could be regulated or reduced by mechanisms such as the balance of power, maintained through diplomacy and strategic alliance.

Modern pioneers of realpolitik

A seminal work in the re-emergence of classical realism in the years between the two world wars was *The Twenty Years' Crisis* (1939) by the British political theorist E. H. Carr. Carr is scathing about utopian (idealist) thinkers who allow dreams of peace and cooperation to blind them to the harsh realities of survival and competition. The leading pioneer in the shift from classical realism to neorealism was the US political theorist Kenneth Waltz. The central thesis of Waltz's *Theory of International Politics* (1979) is that anarchy is the fundamental ordering principle of the 'functionally undifferentiated' states that together make up the international system.

During the Cold War, in a polarized world living under the threat of nuclear annihilation, there was a strong appeal in the stark clarity of the realist world-view, with its unbending focus on security. From the 1970s, however, elegant simplicity began to look like oversimplification, and a more sophisticated version of realism – neorealism – was devised. While this shared many of the assumptions of its classical precursor, it brought a new understanding of the conflict at the heart of the international system, seeing it as a consequence, not of immutable laws of human nature, but of the structure of the system itself.

Being sovereign, the states that constitute the system are formally equal with one another and so do not recognize any authority higher than themselves; the system is thus 'anarchic', in the sense that it lacks any supreme authority to enforce laws and agreements between its members. In such a system, each state is obliged to operate on the principle of 'self-help': in its dealings with other nations, it cannot count on their goodwill but must rely on its own resources to protect its interests.

> **UTOPIA AND REALITY ARE … THE TWO FACETS OF POLITICAL SCIENCE. SOUND POLITICAL THOUGHT AND SOUND POLITICAL LIFE WILL BE FOUND ONLY WHERE BOTH HAVE THEIR PLACE.**
>
> E. H. Carr,
> *The Twenty Years' Crisis,* 1939

COMPLEX INTERDEPENDENCE

Realism, in its neorealist or 'structural' form, remains a highly influential perspective within the study of international relations, not least for the constructive criticism that it has generated. But the strengths of realism – especially its simplicity – are, in the eyes of its critics, its weaknesses. In particular, it is suggested that its state-centred view of the world fails to do justice to the complexity of global relations as they are today. The forces of globalization, economic and other; the influence of transnational and non-state actors (multinational corporations, international organizations, terrorist groups, etc.); the decline and fragmentation of state power; the proliferation of complex threats (terrorist, environmental); the diminished role of conventional military forces: all have conspired to make the realist view appear out of step with current realities. Equally strident have been criticisms of realism's lack of a moral grounding, especially its insistence that conflict is the essential dynamic within the international system. To all of this, the realist would doubtless reply much as he would have done half a century ago: look at the world as it is, not as we might wish it to be.

The condensed idea
The struggle for power

Capitalism

In the days of the Cold War, before the collapse of the communist regimes in the Soviet Union and Eastern Europe that began in 1989, perhaps the best argument in favour of capitalism was that it was not socialism. The futility of socialist attempts to realize an egalitarian society was clear even to those living under communism. 'Under capitalism, man exploits man,' they would joke cynically. 'Under socialism, it's the other way round.'

Following the fall of communism, it was no longer sufficient to be 'less bad' than the alternatives, and the tone adopted by capitalism's supporters became more positive, even triumphalist. In 1992, for instance, the right-wing American commentator Francis Fukuyama predicted that the collapse of authoritarian rule would mark 'the end point of mankind's ideological evolution'; he foresaw the emergence of a 'true global culture ... centering around technologically driven economic growth and the capitalist social relations necessary to produce and sustain it'.

The economic traumas that rocked the world in the early 21st century strained the credibility of this benign vision of capitalism. Indeed, the forces of free-market capitalism were widely blamed for the malaise that reduced many countries to beggary. Capitalism was under scrutiny as never before.

ADAM SMITH AND THE FREE MARKET

Capitalism's admirers tend to present it as an ideology, but in fact it is basically, or at least it was originally, a mode of production: a way of organizing economic

TIMELINE

1776

The principles of free trade are set out in Adam Smith's *The Wealth of Nations*

1867–94

Karl Marx gives his definitive critique of capitalism in *Das Kapital*

activity. The essential features of capitalism are private property, a free market and a framework of laws that allow transactions and contracts to be made. Everything needed to make goods – the 'means of production', such as capital, land, materials and tools – is privately owned by individuals (capitalists), who use them to make things that can be sold at a profit.

Capitalism operates in a market in which goods are freely exchanged. The essential dynamics of the free market were first analysed by the Scottish economist Adam Smith in *The Wealth of Nations* (1776). Smith's genius was to see that, in a pure market where enterprise, competition and motivation towards personal gain are given free rein, the dynamics of supply and demand ensure that producers make goods and provide services that consumers wish to buy, at a price that offers a reasonable return on their investment. The system is naturally self-regulating in that variables such as cost, price and profit are determined as functions of the system as a whole and cannot be manipulated, without undermining the system, either by the parties to a transaction or by any third party outside it.

The implication of Smith's analysis is that decisions of production and distribution should be left to the market, not to government. This is the theoretical justification for the classical liberal doctrine of laissez-faire: the idea that politics and economics are distinct and that politicians should refrain from attempting to direct the course of markets.

The public–private divide

Adam Smith may have claimed that the free market was the most effective means of coordinating economic activity, but he allowed that the state had a role beyond that of merely facilitating commerce. Private entrepreneurs would have no interest in dealing with things in which they could see no profit, so it would always fall to the state to discharge 'the duty of erecting and maintaining certain public works and certain public institutions'. The question whether society's needs, such as transport and education, are best provided by the state or through private initiative has been the subject of fierce debate ever since.

1933

John Maynard Keynes criticizes free trade in his essay 'National Self-Sufficiency'

1989

The state-run (command) economies of the Soviet bloc begin to collapse

2007

Beginning of deep global economic downturn

KARL MARX ON CAPITALIST EXPLOITATION

The modern critique of capitalism takes its lead from the analysis given in the mid-19th century by the German political theorist Karl Marx. For Marx, the origin of capitalism is class conflict between the bourgeoisie (capitalist class), who privately own the means of production, and the proletariat (working class), whose labour is used to generate profit. Capitalism, in Marx's view, is essentially exploitative, because profit is generated precisely by giving workers inadequate reward for their exertions. Thus the wealth created by capitalism could never, even in principle, be shared fairly between worker and employer. Furthermore, capitalism is essentially oppressive, because accumulation of wealth in the hands of the bourgeoisie leads to the concentration of power, not only economic but also social and political, in the same hands.

The exploitation and oppression inherent in capitalism will be brought to an end, Marx argues, only by revolution, in which the bourgeoisie is overthrown and private property abolished. Capitalism will then be replaced by communism, a just system of social organization in which the economy is controlled centrally by the state according to the principle 'from each according to his abilities, to each according to his needs'.

NOT INTELLIGENT, NOT BEAUTIFUL, NOT JUST

Even capitalism's critics do not usually deny its capacity to generate economic growth. In a hundred years of ascendancy, wrote Marx in 1848, the bourgeoisie had 'created more massive and more colossal productive forces than have all preceding generations together'. The main complaint has always been that the distribution of wealth among those involved in generating it is unequal and unfair. Marx's collaborator Friedrich Engels witnessed the misery brought upon working people by the operation of industrial capitalism, in which workers were forced to toil longer for less, in ever more squalid conditions. And in the 20th century the British economist John Maynard Keynes delivered the most damning verdict on the operation of capitalism in the years after the First World War: 'It is not intelligent. It is not beautiful. It is not just. It is not virtuous. And it doesn't deliver the goods.'

THE INVISIBLE HAND

Supporters of capitalism argue that the inequalities it creates are justified because society as a whole is better off under capitalism than it would be

Economics of horse and sparrow

One way in which capitalism's invisible hand was supposed to promote the common interest – at least in the minds of neoliberal champions such as Ronald Reagan and Margaret Thatcher – was the so-called 'trickle-down' effect, in which the greater prosperity of those at the top would filter down to the lower levels, leaving everyone better off than would otherwise be the case. Unfortunately, the usual pattern of history seems to have repeated itself and the rich have continued to get richer and the poor poorer. The theory was magisterially dismissed by the economist J. K. Galbraith as 'horse-and-sparrow economics' – the idea that 'if you feed enough oats to the horse, some will pass through to feed the sparrows'.

under any other system. The self-regulating nature of a free market means that individuals working within it, while acting in their own interest, unconsciously promote the collective good; there is an 'invisible hand', in Adam Smith's phrase, that is responsible for bringing about this benign outcome.

Claiming Smith's authority here is somewhat misleading. The invisible hand, in his account, prompts merchants to promote the public interest by encouraging them to favour *domestic* industry (that is, to invest in their own country), so it would have no such benign effect in an international or global market. The claim that capitalism promotes the global interest is much harder to make. The deep economic damage caused by the reckless greed of international bankers in the early years of the 21st century was but the latest evidence of the trouble that insufficiently regulated capitalist institutions can bring.

The lack of a viable alternative may still be the best argument for capitalism, but the full-blooded, libertarian, 'small-state' variant that demands that governments keep their hands off at all times is hard to sustain. The question now, most agree, is not whether the state should intervene in markets, but how much and how often.

The condensed idea
The triumph of greed?

48 Lifeboat Earth

The distribution of wealth across the face of the Earth is extremely uneven – and, one might say, extremely unfair. At the turn of the 21st century it was estimated that 85 per cent of the world's assets belonged to just one-tenth of the population. The poorer half of the world's inhabitants, meanwhile, owned just 1 per cent of global wealth. In impoverished parts of the world, hundreds of millions of people do not have adequate shelter or access to safe water or basic health services, while over 10 million children under the age of five die each year of malnutrition and preventable diseases.

So, vast wealth on one side and dire poverty on the other. Those lucky enough to be on the right side of the divide do not do nothing, of course – many billions of dollars of international aid are given annually by richer countries to poorer. But is it enough? Anyone with a conscience, living in comfort and luxury unimaginable to most people in the world, cannot fail to wonder occasionally if they are falling short in their moral duty to their fellow humans.

ADRIFT IN A MORAL SEA

Well, not quite *everyone*, perhaps. In a paper published in 1974, the US ecologist Garrett Hardin argues that we in the West are actually doing too much for people in poorer parts of the world. To explain why, he introduces his now-famous metaphor of Lifeboat Earth:

TIMELINE

1968

Garrett Hardin develops the idea of the tragedy of the commons

1974

Hardin's paper 'Living on a lifeboat' is published

So here we sit, say 50 people in our lifeboat. To be generous, let us assume it has room for 10 more, making a total capacity of 60. Suppose the 50 of us in the lifeboat see 100 others swimming in the water outside, begging for admission to our boat or for handouts. We have several options: we may be tempted to try to live by the Christian ideal of being 'our brother's keeper', or by the Marxist ideal of 'to each according to his needs'. Since the needs of all in the water are the same, and since they can all be seen as 'our brothers', we could take them all into our boat, making a total of 150 in a boat designed for 60. The boat swamps, everyone drowns. Complete justice, complete catastrophe.

Better not to admit any onto the lifeboat – that is the surest means of surviving ourselves, 'although we shall have to be constantly on guard against boarding parties'.

Hardin's picture is not pretty: the rich safely ensconced in their boats and using their oars to crack the knuckles of the poor as they attempt to climb on board. However, his position, while attacked by critics as lacking in compassion, is not obviously immoral. After all, Hardin believes that the West's interventions are damaging to *both* sides, however well-intentioned they may be. Countries on the receiving end of foreign aid develop a culture of dependence and so fail to 'learn the hard way' the dangers of inadequate forward planning. In particular, thanks to the safety net of Western aid, they do not immediately suffer the horrors of uncontrolled population growth, but in this way the harsh day of reckoning is merely postponed to generations to come. At the same time, unrestricted immigration means that near-stagnant Western populations rapidly become swamped by an unstoppable tide of economic refugees.

> **FOR THE FORESEEABLE FUTURE SURVIVAL DEMANDS THAT WE GOVERN OUR ACTIONS BY THE ETHICS OF A LIFEBOAT. POSTERITY WILL BE ILL SERVED IF WE DO NOT.**
> Garrett Hardin, 1974

2008

The number of humanitarian aid workers is estimated at over 200,000

2009

The United Nations reports that 17,000 children die of hunger every day

The tragedy of the commons

Hardin's 'toughlove' lifeboat ethics was a direct response to what he saw as the shortcomings of the cosy spaceship Earth metaphor beloved of head-in-the-clouds liberals. The liberal's cherished image of one big, happy crew all working together encourages the view that the world's resources should be held in common and that everyone must have a fair and equal share of them. A farmer who owns a piece of land will look after his property and ensure that it is not ruined by overgrazing, but if it becomes common ground open to all, there will not be the same concern to protect it. The temptations of short-term gain mean that voluntary restraint soon evaporates, and degradation and decline rapidly follow. This process – inevitable, in Hardin's view, in 'a crowded world of less than perfect human beings' – is what he calls the 'tragedy of the commons'. In just this way, when the Earth's resources, such as air, water and the fish of the oceans, are treated as commons, there is no proper stewardship of them and ruin is sure to follow.

Unapologetic about his harsh lifeboat ethics, Hardin himself has no doubt where to lay the blame: the 'bleeding-heart' liberals whose over-active consciences prompt them to ill-conceived humanitarian action. His advice to these guilt-stricken liberals is to 'get out and yield your place to others', thereby eliminating feelings of remorse that threaten to destabilize the boat. There is no point worrying about how we got here – 'we cannot remake the past'; it's safeguarding the world for future generations that should concern us.

LIBERALS AND SPACESHIP EARTH

Hardin's 'toughlove' solution to world poverty is doubtless especially objectionable to liberals, who are typically disinclined to clubbing anyone over the head with an oar. One of the basic requirements of social justice, in the liberal view, is that people are treated impartially: things beyond our control, such as our gender and skin colour, should not be allowed to determine how we are treated. We have no control over where we are born, so no moral weight should be attached to national boundaries.

Hardin, of course, may wearily observe that this is exactly the kind of social justice that is sure to send the boat to the bottom of the ocean. But the liberal does not have to accept Hardin's interpretation. Is the lifeboat really in danger of sinking? Is it not perhaps the case that the fat cats, over-used to onboard luxury, need to budge up a bit and take a cut in their rations? For instance – the liberal might object – Hardin assumes that high reproductive rates are a constant feature of poorer countries and would persist even if they got a fairer deal. He does not allow for the possibility that such rates are a *response* to high infant mortality, low life expectancy, poor education, and so on.

Indeed, liberals are likely to reject the lifeboat metaphor altogether. Their preferred image is 'spaceship Earth'. We are all on board spaceship Earth together, and it is our duty to ensure that we take care of the ship and do not waste its precious resources. To this end, it is essential that all the crew work together – and they won't do that unless they are satisfied that they are getting their fair share of the ship's rations.

DOES MORALITY RECOGNIZE BORDERS?

Liberals may believe that they live on spaceship Earth. The problem is that most of them, most of the time, do not behave as if they do. In practice, the requirements of social justice seem to stop at national boundaries, or at least become highly diluted in the process of crossing. No developed country does a *fraction* of what would be necessary in order to eradicate the gross inequalities that exist in the world today. And it is not only followers of Garrett Hardin who are sitting pretty in their luxury cabins while the rest of the world sinks around them.

To avoid the charge of hypocrisy, liberals are bound to show why the demands of impartiality can be suspended or diluted when they consider parts of the world other than their own. Or they should accept that current practices and policies are inadequate and embrace a full-blown cosmopolitan liberalism in which the principles of social justice are extended globally. Some philosophers have attempted to address these issues, and a few have called for a radical sea-change, both in theory and in practice. But they have only scratched the tip of the iceberg – and the lifeboat is approaching fast, on full collision course.

The condensed idea
All adrift in a moral sea

Poverty

Poverty is not inevitable. It exists because the vital resources that sustain human life are not evenly distributed. There are enough of these resources that everyone alive today could live a tolerably comfortable life. The fact that resources are unequally allocated is the result not of natural necessity but of human choice. Whether there should be a more equal, or less unequal, distribution is a key concern of social justice.

In broad terms, poverty is a condition in which people are unable to satisfy their basic needs and hence to function normally within society. But what counts as basic and what counts as normal? In economically developed countries, poverty is usually considered in *relative* terms: people are considered poor not because they lack the basic requirements needed to sustain life, but because they fall below a minimum standard that is set relative to others in the community. In many developing countries, by contrast, a significant proportion of the population live in *absolute* poverty: they live at or near the subsistence level, with barely enough food to keep themselves alive.

RELATIVE POVERTY AND THE DEVELOPED WORLD

The total wealth generated by an industrialized economy is such that, if it were divided up more equally among all members of society, nobody would be poor, in relative or absolute terms. So why is it allowed to continue?

From a socialist perspective poverty is a structural feature of capitalism and is never justified: the goal of maximizing profit entails exploiting the labour force through low wages, thereby increasing inequality and hence (relative)

TIMELINE

1972	1974
Peter Singer argues, in 'Famine, affluence, and morality', that current levels of international aid are grotesquely inadequate	Garrett Hardin's article 'Living on a lifeboat' suggests that aid is counterproductive

poverty. Socialism, therefore, sets out to eradicate poverty by reallocating resources in order to create equality of social and economic conditions.

The classical liberal view also sees poverty as structural, but it shares little else with the socialist analysis. Its central assumption is that the distribution of resources within the state is determined most efficiently by market forces. Within a free market, individuals compete with one another in pursuit of their own interest, thereby producing an economic outcome that is better than any alternative but not equally good for all – there are always winners and losers. The resulting pattern of wealth is a reflection of the talents and skills of individuals; wealth provides a motivation to succeed, while fear of poverty is one of the incentives that drive individual effort and enterprise.

All modern liberal democracies profess to be capitalist, but in practice none of them believes that it is right to entrust the well-being of its citizens entirely to the whim of the market. A just social organization requires that all members have an equal opportunity to promote their interests, even if some inevitably make more of that opportunity than others. Views differ on how much should be done to level the playing field – and in reality every field remains very bumpy – but all agree that some amount of state intervention is necessary to mitigate the poverty and other ills that would be created by unrestrained capitalism.

ABSOLUTE POVERTY AND THE DEVELOPING WORLD

It is conceivable that supporters of capitalism, living in relative poverty, might regard their condition as tolerable because they believe in the system

The poverty line

The poverty line, which serves as a measure of relative poverty in developed countries, generally indicates that a household has insufficient resources, in terms of income, to participate in the social and leisure activities typically enjoyed by other households within the community. Thus, for example, in a society where the possession of a television or a telephone is considered normal and necessary, the fact of being unable to afford them may be taken as an indication of poverty.

2000

The United Nations Millennium Declaration pledges to eradicate extreme poverty by 2015

2012

The IMF database indicates that the richest country is 292 times richer than the poorest

Spreading the blame

A common way of excusing our own inactivity when it comes to relieving the great suffering caused by world poverty is to point to all the others who are no less inactive. But the fact that others fail to act as they should does not make it right for you to do so: if a child was drowning in a pond, it would not make it less blameworthy for you to let it happen just because others were standing around doing nothing. It is true that, if everyone in the affluent parts of the world gave a few hundred dollars to relieve poverty, poverty could be largely eradicated overnight. But that is not the real world, and in the real world – where most people give nothing – it may be our moral duty to give a great deal more than our 'fair share'.

that gives rise to that condition and offers them the best chance (so they suppose) of escaping from it. This could never be the case with absolute poverty, which is invariably a wretched affliction that blights and often ends lives.

The gulf between rich and poor countries in the world today is vast. According to figures produced by the International Monetary Fund in 2012, the richest country in the world, Qatar, is 292 times richer than the poorest, the Democratic Republic of Congo (the USA is 136 times richer). Wealth is mainly concentrated in North America, Europe and a few other areas, while poverty is widespread, especially in South Asia and Africa. While many billions of dollars are donated annually by rich countries to poor ones, the amount given in aid is nowhere near sufficient to redress the balance, and for the most part the gap between rich and poor is growing wider.

HARDIN VERSUS SINGER

A case can be made for saying that no aid should be given to poorer, developing countries. An influential advocate of such a view was the US ecologist Garrett Hardin, who argued that countries bailed out by foreign aid were prevented from learning the lessons of their own imprudence (in particular, the folly of uncontrolled population growth), and hence that handouts from rich countries merely shifted current problems to succeeding generations (*see chapter 48*).

There is a powerful argument on the other side, most famously made by the Australian ethicist Peter Singer, which suggests that current levels of international aid are grossly inadequate. Singer's argument is based on two assumptions:

1 Suffering and death from lack of food, shelter and medical care are bad.
2 If it is in our power to prevent something bad from happening,

without thereby sacrificing anything of comparable moral importance, we ought, morally, to do it.

Singer supposes that both of these assumptions will generally be accepted, though he offers the following case in support of the second:

> If I am walking past a shallow pond and see a child drowning in it, I ought to wade in and pull the child out. This will mean getting my clothes muddy, but this is insignificant, while the death of the child would presumably be a very bad thing.

Here, the moral duty to make a sacrifice (in this case, a very small one: to mess up my clothes) in order to save a life seems obvious. There may be disagreement, in practice, about what counts as 'anything of comparable moral importance', but it would be hard to argue that my having a new sports car or the latest iPod is morally as significant as saving another human being from the ravages of poverty. Singer's argument suggests that, at the very least, we should give up the innumerable luxuries that are now taken for granted in developed countries.

A NEW MORAL OUTLOOK

In fact, Singer believes that we should give up a great deal more than just luxuries – even though to spend on foreign aid what we currently spend on things that we do not really need would in itself represent a revolution in the way we lead our lives. Indeed, accepting his argument would require a transformation of our whole moral outlook, as the traditional line between duty and charity would be erased. With regard to the absolute poverty that exists in the world today, the uncomfortable conclusion is that the one position that is impossible to defend is the one in which we currently find ourselves.

The condensed idea
Rich and poor – a world divided

50 The environment

There is only one Earth. For the foreseeable future, this planet will be our only home, and our survival depends on its continuing ability to provide us with food and other resources. Throughout history the Earth has met these needs, but in recent times the burden placed on it has increased dramatically and there have been growing concerns over its ability to cope with the impact of human activity. The need to reassess our relationship with the Earth and the value we attach to all of its contents has given new urgency to the study of environmental ethics.

For every person on Earth in the early 1700s, there are more than 11 alive today, each one of whom makes (on average) a far greater demand on the finite resources available. Human ingenuity has devised new ways to meet growing demands on already depleted resources, but industrialization across the globe has greatly magnified mankind's capacity to damage natural systems. The strains on the planet cannot continue to grow indefinitely: the energy-hungry lifestyles widely adopted in the West are unsustainable.

For most of human history, attitudes to animals and plants and to the natural world in general have been exploitative. Humans have tended to behave as if the planet were something to be conquered and tamed – an asset to be exploited, a resource to be plundered. This view was supported by the Bible and further corroborated by the ancient Greeks, and in particular Aristotle, who believed that humans stood at the end of a 'chain of being' and that it was the function of lower animals to serve those higher in the hierarchy.

TIMELINE

1700	1960s
World population is at an estimated 0.6 billion	First warnings that human activity might contribute to global warming

The non-identity problem

Suppose that we are debating, as a society, whether to live it up now or save for the future: to deplete or conserve the various resources available to us. And suppose, too, that the depletion option means that people alive now and over the next century will enjoy a slightly higher quality of life but those living thereafter, for many centuries, will have a much poorer quality of life. Surely this scenario gives us some moral reason not to choose the depletion option? But the choice we make now will make all sorts of differences, not least to the circumstances and timing of human conceptions. The future people who will suffer as a result of our choice to deplete owe their very existence to that same choice. We may think that depleting resources is wrong because it harms these future people, but actually it does not harm anyone: assuming that their lives are worth living, these people should be glad that we chose as we did, for otherwise they would not have existed at all. This paradoxical conclusion is an example of the so-called non-identity problem, discussed by the British philosopher Derek Parfit in his 1984 book *Reasons and Persons*. Parfit's argument perhaps says more about the nature of wrong actions than it does about the rights and wrongs of depleting resources.

ENLIGHTENED STEWARDSHIP

Many pioneers of the modern green movement, which began in the late 1960s, were motivated primarily by the dangers posed to humans by their abusive treatment of the planet. They did not necessarily challenge the human-centred (anthropocentric) focus of traditional attitudes, and their concerns were often expressed in terms of our responsibilities to fellow humans and to future generations. The favoured image was one of 'enlightened stewardship', in which a properly developed ecological consciousness, allied to prudence and self-interest, counselled respectful and sustainable management of our fragile planet.

The pragmatic aspect of this approach was reflected in the 1987 report *Our Common Future*, produced by the World Commission on the Environment

1992

Sustainability is discussed at the first UN Earth Summit, in Rio de Janeiro, Brazil

2012

World population exceeds 7 billion

and Development. Here, sustainability was defined as 'development that meets the needs of the present without compromising the ability of future generations to meet their own needs'. The report recognized that there was a better prospect of changing human behaviour than human nature, and it did not suggest that 'the needs of the present' were simply misguided. Indeed, it anticipated 'the possibility of a new era of economic growth, based on policies that sustain and expand the natural environmental resource base'. The message was not that we have to abandon all our existing aspirations but that we have to be smarter and more sympathetic in realizing them.

A part, not apart

Environmentalists are generally in agreement on the remedy to our current ills: sustainable development. According to this model, all economic (and other) activity must take full account of its toll on the environment and so avoid environmental degradation and long-term depletion of natural resources. We save ourselves by saving the planet, and this calls for changes in attitude. 'We abuse land because we regard it as a commodity belonging to us,' wrote US ecologist Aldo Leopold in his influential *A Sand County Almanac* (1949). 'When we see land as a community to which we belong, we may begin to use it with love and respect.'

DEEP ECOLOGY

There have always been other, more strident voices that have called for a transformation of our relationship with the environment. From this radical perspective, known as 'deep ecology', the image of the sympathetic steward is rejected as implying an unequal and exploitative relationship between humans and nature.

The central claim of deep ecologists is that non-human animals, plants and the other components of the environment are intrinsically valuable, not just instrumentally as the means to some human benefit. The Earth and all its teeming life are not worthy of our consideration because (or *merely* because) they serve our needs or are beautiful and enrich our lives. Indeed, many of the species that share the planet with us are neither useful nor beautiful, yet they are still inherently valuable. Our moral obligations therefore extend beyond our fellow human beings, present and future, to encompass other forms of life and the world itself. It is simply not enough to save the Earth in order to save ourselves: we need to live in harmony with nature because we are not apart from it but part of it.

Whatever the attractions of deep ecology, it is not without its difficulties. We may suppose that moral consideration is due to things that have interests or feelings, and that the amount of consideration should be proportionate to the degree of sentience that a thing has. On this basis we may regard many or most non-human animals as deserving some amount of moral respect. But what are the interests of a tree? Or, still more oddly, of an inanimate object such as a stream or a mountain? Even allowing that we can make sense of the idea that everything in nature has intrinsic value, we may wonder how much moral respect we, as humans, should give to a malarial mosquito or a smallpox virus – even though they, like us, may have interests of their own. Deep ecology quickly takes on a mystical aspect, which is doubtless part of its attraction, but such mysticism may sometimes appear to hide a basic incoherence.

WITH OR WITHOUT US

One of the most influential elaborations of deep ecology is the Gaia theory, first proposed by the British independent scientist James Lovelock in his 1979 book *Gaia: A New Look at Life on Earth*. Lovelock's central idea is that life on Earth maintains the conditions necessary for its own survival: our 'stable planet made of unstable parts' is kept in a state of equilibrium by gigantic feedback mechanisms driven by the combined regulatory activity of all its living and non-living components. Humans may be parts and partners of the whole, but they are 'just another species, neither the owners nor the stewards of this planet'. The lesson of Gaia is that the health of our world depends on taking a planetary perspective. The ominous implication is that the Earth is likely to survive, however badly we treat it, but that its survival does not necessarily include us.

The condensed idea
Saving ourselves, saving the planet

Glossary

absolutism The view that there are moral standards that can never be broken, such that certain actions are right or wrong whatever the consequences.

altruism Disinterested or selfless regard for the welfare of others.

anti-realism *see* subjectivism.

autonomy The capacity of a moral agent to exercise full and independent control over his or her actions.

consequentialism The view that the rightness of actions should be assessed purely by reference to their effectiveness in bringing about certain desirable ends or states of affairs.

cynicism Informally, a tendency or disposition to doubt the sincerity or goodness of human actions and motives.

deontology The view that certain actions are intrinsically right or wrong, irrespective of their consequences; particular emphasis is placed on the duties and intentions of moral agents.

determinism The theory that every event has a prior cause, and hence that every state of the world is necessitated or determined by a previous state.

dilemma Informally, a choice between two alternatives (the 'horns' of the dilemma), neither of which is attractive or favourable.

dogmatism Insistence on the truth of certain principles, often with a concomitant unwillingness to consider the views of others.

duty Something that one is obliged to do, or that is owed (due) to other people. The idea of duty or obligation is the central idea of deontological approaches to ethics (*see* deontology).

egoism The view that people are, as a matter of fact, motivated by self-interest (psychological egoism) or that they should be so motivated (ethical egoism).

emotivism Broadly, the view that ethical statements are expressions of a speaker's emotional states, rather than claims that may be true or false.

empirical Describing a concept or belief that is based on experience.

Enlightenment The 'Age of Reason', the period of Western historical thought, beginning in the late 17th century and driven by the Scientific Revolution, in which the power of reason was elevated over the authority of religion and tradition.

fatalism The view that whatever will be will be and hence that it makes no difference how we act.

free will *see under* determinism.

humanism Any view in which human affairs are accorded primary importance; in particular, the Renaissance movement in which human dignity was elevated over religious dogma.

intuitionism The view that moral claims are objectively right or wrong and can be known only by a special faculty known as 'intuition'.

Kantian Concerning or connected to Immanuel Kant (1724–1804) or his philosophical views.

liberalism A political philosophy that prioritizes the individual as the bearer of a range of rights and liberties against the power of the state.

materialism A tendency to hold material possessions and physical comforts above spiritual values.

meritocracy A social system in which power or status is granted in proportion to merit (talent and effort) , rather than as a consequence of class, gender, age, etc.

natural law The idea that there is an order in nature from which humans can rationally derive standards or rules of human conduct; it is generally supposed to provide the permanent foundation of humanly constructed laws.

naturalism The view that moral concepts can be explained or analysed purely in terms of 'facts of nature' that are in principle discoverable by science.

neo-liberalism An economic and political theory that combines aspects of classical liberalism (especially the omnipotence of free markets) with an enthusiasm for personal liberty and shrinking the state.

normative Relating to the norms (standards or principles) by which human conduct is judged or directed.

objectivism The view that values and properties such as goodness and beauty are inherent in, or intrinsic to, objects and exist independently of human apprehension of them.

obligation *see* duty.

paternalism The tendency or policy of an authority such as the state to limit the liberties of subordinates or dependants in what it considers to be their best interests.

plagiarism The practice of claiming, or passing off, someone else's work as one's own.

pluralism A form of tolerance of different view, cultures, etc., based on the assumption that no one such view or culture is superior to another.

pragmatism The view that beliefs or principles should be evaluated by how successful they are in practice.

rationalism Broadly, the insistence that action and opinion should be based on reason and knowledge; a frequent contrast is with faith or belief founded on religious revelation or tradition.

realism The view that values and properties really exist 'out there' in the world, independently of our knowing or experiencing them.

Reformation A religious movement in 16th-century Europe that called for reform of the Roman Catholic Church and led to the emergence of Protestantism.

relativism The view that the rightness or wrongness of actions is determined by, or relative to, the culture and traditions of particular social groups or communities.

Renaissance A revival of European art and literature, lasting from the 14th to 16th centuries, that was inspired by rediscovery of classical models.

scepticism A philosophical position that challenges or questions our claims to knowledge in ethics and other areas of discourse.

secularism The view that human well-being in the present life should be the basis of morality, to the exclusion of all religious considerations.

subjectivism The view that value is grounded not in external reality but in our beliefs about it or emotional responses to it (*see also* emotivism).

utilitarianism An ethical system in which actions are judged right or wrong to the extent that they increase or decrease human well-being or 'utility'; utility is classically interpreted as human pleasure or happiness.

Index

In working on this book I have been especially indebted to Chad Vance, graduate instructor at the University of Colorado, whose wisdom, generously shared, has greatly improved the selection of topics and many of the articles: his students are fortunate to have him.

Quercus Editions Ltd
55 Baker Street
7th Floor, South Block
London
W1U 8EW

First published in 2013

A catalogue record of this book is available from the British Library

UK and associated territories:
ISBN 978 1 78087 827 0

Printed and bound in China

10 9 8 7 6 5 4 3 2 1